GREAT MONOLOGUES IN DIALECT FOR YOUNG ACTORS (AGES 17 - 25)

Volume II

GREAT MONOLOGUES IN DIALECT FOR YOUNG ACTORS (AGES 17 - 25)

Volume II

Edited and with a Foreword
by Kimberly Mohne Hill

Smith and Kraus Publishers

For Kristin and Kenzie . . .
may you one day
travel to these places
and hear these sounds in person!

It is hard to believe that ten years have passed since the publishing of the first series of Dialect books (*Great Scenes in Dialect for Young Actors* and *Great Monologues in Dialect for Young Actors*)! The books have served as a reference point and a useful classroom tool for teachers and actors alike, and it gives me great pleasure to bring volume two to you.

As time passes, more plays are written and more topics become popular for theatrical introspection. In collecting the monologues for this edition of the anthologies, it was important to include the latest issues and the broadest palette of characters for the actors to play. *It is important to note that the themes and language of some of these selections are for mature actors and may require some classroom management with what we call "difficult conversations."* This may be especially true in some Southern monologues where the literature uses difficult words in era-specific circumstances. Care and sensitivity on the part of the actors and directors is required. There are strong emotional topics represented in many of the monologues, and, especially in the African Continent section, there are some very dramatic situations. There are not many comic pieces here. I'm not sure why it turned out that way, but perhaps it is appropriate to have advanced to more complex material in a "Volume II."

The monologues in volume two are taken from the five major dialect regionalisms to be studied: British, Irish, Latina/o, African Continent, and American South. While the plays represented in the selections *can* use the dialects of the region in question, it is also possible that *no* dialect is required by the author. The monologue selections are meant to serve as an in-depth study into the literature, environment, culture, and language of a region and may not necessarily be performed in dialect in a non-classroom situation.

In the ten years since the first series of books was published, many things have changed. The first books listed film and television programs as resources for the collection of "sound samples" on which to base a dialect choice. There was also mention of a brand new website called the *International Dialects of English Archive*. This website now contains hundreds of samples of native speakers from all over the globe. The biggest change that has had the most profound effect on the research and study of dialects, however, has been the advancement of internet sources. When *YouTube* was founded in 2005, the ability to stream videos and podcasts from people around the world enabled researchers and actors to acquire first-hand dialect samples of any dialect they wished instantaneously.

Another exciting and notable advancement in the world of dialect study, is the current popularity of collecting "Oral Narratives" (also available instantly online). The BBC began a "Voices" project which allowed for the recording of people all across Great Britain. Those interviews were transcribed and posted on the *BBC Voices* website, and we now have instant access to the vast and varied sounds which occur in Great Britain. Beyond the BBC, the *Library of Congress* is now also a repository for online websites which offer digital archives of recorded interviews of Americans around a variety of themes. There are interviews and narratives with veterans of the World Wars, immigrants discussing their experiences, former southern slave narratives and interviews with survivors of 9/11, among many others. These collections are free and accessible to anyone with a computer and internet access.

As a Dialect Coach, the existence of these websites brings me great excitement. When I have to research a dialect, I go to the internet in a sort of "treasure hunt" mode—hoping to come upon the most recent or most obscure collection of oral narratives that I can bring to my actors and clients! I encourage my students, when they are studying dialect with me, to go out into the world and seek out their own subjects for their own interviews. With this approach, the students can put a real, human connection behind the sounds and rhythms of the dialect being studied, and they can remember that, as actors, we are charged with bringing that humanity to life . . . not just to replicate sounds.

To that end, it is my hope that upon the acquiring of this book, you will use the monologues as a springboard for the discovery of the human being you are called to represent in the playing of the character. Find out about that person. Discover what your character likes to eat, to read, to see on a daily basis. What is their heart's desire? Where do they live? Why do they have this story to tell?

When you dive into the discovery of your characters in such a deep and committed way, it enables you to embrace every aspect of the character—the way they move, the way they gesture, and, of course, the way they talk. Dialect choices become more than just slapping on some sounds at the end of your process, dialect comes from the soul of the character—from the life history of the character, not from a sheet of paper your dialect coach handed you at the first rehearsal. When you approach dialect studies in this way, your character will sound real, truthful, and specific. If you approach dialect as an afterthought, you may be setting yourself up for a stereotypical, shallow character. Be careful.

Though each dialect represented in this book has been given a title and a definition of locale/region (British, Irish, etc.), it is important to note that the sound samples represented are a collection of sounds that *could* exist in each area, but *do not* represent the sounds of *all* the speakers in all the areas discussed. These chapters are not to be taken as a "standard" accent for any of those regions. It is up to you, the actor, to research the local specifics of the dialect your character speaks and to use the sound change charts as a *note-taking device* to help you organize your process. Listen to native sources of the dialect you require and use the dialect chapters in this book as a quick way to find the specific changes required by your character. Highlight those changes only, and then you will have your own, character specific, dialect sound change chart.

Keep in mind, when looking at the sound change charts, that I have begun each change with a "base" sound and then I have an arrow that points to what the sound becomes in the dialect. The "base" sound represented is a General American English (GAE) pronunciation (probably with a bit of a California flair since I am from California). If you are from another part of the country or world, please note that the first sound you see on the sound change charts may not be the way that you say that sound. I needed to use *someone's* dialect as a base, so I used mine!

To the actor, teacher or coach that uses this book—thank you! I hope you find the acting selections challenging, fun and inspiring and I hope that the dialect information serves to help you on your way to a deeper understanding of your character's rich regionally-specific history.

Kimberly Mohne Hill

BRITISH

STANDARD BRITISH DIALECT

(a.k.a. Received Pronunciation/RP)

Every year, either for a scene study class or a fully staged production, I am asked to coach a Standard British dialect. Quite often this request will come up more than once in a season. By sheer numbers this seems to be the dialect that most American actors will need to acquire. If you can begin to work on the dialect before you even get the part, you will be miles ahead of everyone else. Your comfort with the dialect will show in the confidence of your performance.

It is important to know that there exists in Britain (and indeed in each area of dialect we will study) a wide variety of dialects which are based upon the region's economic, social and geographic conditions. For example, in the western coastal region of England, the accent of the people of Liverpool is influenced by the proximity (across the water) of its Irish neighbors which creates a speech pattern that can sound completely different than the one heard in London. As an actor, it is up to you to find out where your character is from, and research the dialect needs of that particular region. The BBC Voices Project website is an excellent resource for this type of research.

The people of England can tend to be very class-conscious and focus intently on their speech as a symbol of their status in the community at large. Most British school children have undergone some form of speech training or elocution. This may or may not have been embraced by the student—resulting in either an RP accent [a "standard," non-region-specific British accent called Received Pronunciation] that draws little attention to one's regional/social roots, or a complete rejection of the RP sounds and an embracing of one's regional/social dialect. Today, the RP dialect is undergoing a transformation due to the embracing of regional sounds. The Cockney dialect, for example, has begun to "cross the river" (the estuary) and affect the Standard London sound, creating an amalgam called "Estuary English" which is not as formal sounding as RP. At any rate, for many people in Britain, speech and dialect hold a personal meaning.

As mentioned in the Introduction to the book, however, keep in mind that acting in dialect does not simply mean changing your sounds; it means altering your entire carriage. This is especially true when acting 'British'. American actors who begin to study a British dialect often conclude that they must act "high status," almost snobby, when they adopt a British sound. Some have been known to speak in flippant tones with chins and noses up-raised and in a manner which actually pokes fun at the dialect when it should be embraced for all its subtle and relaxed nuances. Fortunately, we have a plethora of fabulous British films and actors to serve as primary source material for study. This access to popular British media sources allows actors to train their ears to hear the British sound and rhythm in its native source/environment. Surrounding oneself with the influences of native British speakers will enable the actor to move beyond the cliché into the adoption of a truthful and well-placed dialect.

What follows are some tips about the dialect and the important sound changes/elements of a Standard British/RP Dialect. Remember, in order to adopt a more regional British sound, you will have to research the specific region and its sounds and rhythms.

Mouth/Physical Thoughts:

● As an American (Californian) actor doing a British dialect, I have noticed that I must make my mouth rounder than it normally is—indeed, when I look at British people speaking, the corners of their mouths seem to come closer together in an almost "frowning" way. That is not to say that British people do not smile, they do, but the placement of their sound has an element of roundness to it quite consistently.

● Because of the roundness of the lips, the sound of the dialect feels more like it is in the front of the mouth. There is still great openness and roundness at the base of the tongue near the throat, as well. I like to imagine the sounds coming out already formed perfectly way down in the center of my body.

Sound/Music Thoughts:

● Tom Stoppard (author of *Arcadia, Rosencrantz & Guildenstern are Dead, Shakespeare in Love*) visited A.C.T. (American Conservatory Theater) once and gave a brief talk to the students there. One student asked him what was needed when performing a Stoppard play. His response: "clarity of utterance." This precision about the British sounds requires some conscious effort, but must appear to be completely easy and relaxed when speaking.

● The British dialect tends to stress only one syllable per word and ignore the rest. For example, we (in California) say "SEK ra tair ree" (secretary) and they would say "SEK ruh trih." We tend to pay attention to every syllable of a word while they focus on the stressed syllable only.

● If a word is unimportant in a sentence (usually articles, conjunctions, pronouns, linking verbs), the British barely give it any notice at all. They isolate the image words and the operative (important) words of the sentence, which helps with the British rhythm.

● Even though the British speaker has a different inflection rhythm when s/he asks a question (s/he tends to raise and then lower and then raise slightly the pitch and inflection on the second to last word/syllable in the sentence, i.e. "Do you WANT some?"), it is important to keep the inflection under check so as not to become too sing-song. Just remind yourself to *mean* what you say.

ACTING THOUGHTS:

● We *like* hearing them talk. There is a reason for that. They know how to make speech sound eloquent and flawless. As a teacher reminded me once, "they invented the language!" There is power to that awareness—you can *know* people will listen to you! You don't need to add all your "American" facial/hand gestures to punctuate your sound—just use the music of your voice.

● Please do not use your new British dialect on Shakespeare. It is a "bad acting" cliché.

Standard British Dialect Sounds/Elements

Vowel/Diphthong Changes:

● The Dropped "R": The British dialect drops the [r] sound at the ends of words and when the [r] precedes a consonant. The [uh] you see in the substitutions below is actually really subtle. It's a little off-glide of sound. Pay attention to the first part of the change (the pure vowel) and the rest should take care of itself. If you overdo the [uh] sound, you might go towards a Brooklyn dialect, so be careful! Keep the "essence of 'r'" in there and pretend you are still saying it.

ear →	ih_{uh}	here, we're, dear	→	hih_{uh}, wih_{uh}, dih_{uh}
air →	eh_{uh}	where, their, fare	→	weh_{uh}, $theh_{uh}$, feh_{uh}
oor →	oo_{uh}	sure, boor, moor	→	$shoo_{uh}$, boo_{uh}, moo_{uh}
ore →	oh_{uh}	you're, more, door	→	yoh_{uh}, moh_{uh}, doh_{uh}
are →	ah	far, car, yard	→	fah, kah, yahd
er →	eh/uh	early, girl, word, heard	→	ehly, gehl, wuh-d, huh-d

● The Intrusive "R": You may have heard the insertion of an [r] in words where there is no[r] . . . for example "the idea[r] of one's happiness . . . " (*Sense & Sensibility*, Emma Thompson). This happens when a word ends with an [uh] sound and the next word starts with a vowel. This is an "overcompensation" for the "linking [r]" rule. Usage of this dialect substitution will depend on your character's circumstances and your director's choice.

● The "Round Sounds": These will take some effort and an ear in order for you to hear the difference. Most Americans do not make these sounds naturally (except the Brooklyn/New Yorkers) and so you will have to retrain your mouth and your mind to get them to be natural. You must really round your lips and drop your jaw open (two fingers wide) in order to shape these sounds . . . but remember to imagine the sound coming out from the center of your body already perfectly rounded.

Kimberly Mohne Hill　　23

oh → ₚ*oh*/ₑₕ*oh*   *go, slow, road, show*   →   *g*ₚₕ*oh, sl*ₚₕ*oh, r*ₚₕ*ohd, sh*ₚₕ*oh*
(a quick little [uh] or [eh] glide into the [oh] sound)

ah → *or*   *saw, awesome, hall*   →   *sor, orsome, horl*
(rounded almost to an "oh" or "oo" sound—start the word as if you are going to
say "or," but then drop the "r")

ah → *o*   *hot, top, stop, not*   →   *hot, top, stop, not*
(rounded and "popped" off the back of your tongue, like the sound in the word
"pop")

ow →   *ah oo*   *how, found, crown*   →   *hah oo, fah oond, crah oon*
(still present in RP, but beginning to relax a little . . . very open, rounded [ah] into
the [ow] sound)

● The "Liquid U": Much the way the word "music" has
  a [y] sound after the consonant [m], the British dialect
  inserts a [y] sound before the long [u] sound after the
  letters [t], [d] and [n]. Note: if the word has an [o] in the
  spelling, do not use the Liquid [u].

Duke, duty, dubious	→	*Dyuke, dyutih, dyubious*
new, pneumonia, nuisance	→	*nyew, nyumonia, nyusance*
tune, Tuesday, tutor	→	*tyune, Tyusedih, tyutuh*

● The "Bright ă" sound (formerly called the "pure Anne
  sound"): American actors will tend to blend the short [ă]
  in the word into the consonant which follows it in a word
  which changes the [ă] into an [ay] sound. For example,
  one may hear "baynk" instead of "b ă nk" or "care ee"
  instead of "c ă ree" (carry). In the British dialect, you
  must *pay attention to the vowel* (all vowels) before you
  move on to the consonant. The [a] sound is made with
  a wide open, smiling mouth (like you are biting into an
  apple). Make the vowel sound purely, and *then* say the
  consonant that follows it.

    stand, carry, arrow, marriage → *stand, carry, arrow, marriage*

- Prefixes/Suffixes: Keeping with the tradition of stressing only one syllable in a word and "clarity of utterance," the British dialect uses the pure, short sound [ih] on prefixes/suffixes where we, especially in California, would say [ee] or [ed].

believe, prepare, rehearse → *b$_{ih}$ lieve, pr$_{ih}$ pehuh, r$_{ih}$ hehse*

wanted, lovely, wordy → *wan t$_{ih}$d, love l$_{ih}$, wuh d$_{ih}$*

- Special pronunciations: Many words would seem to be pronounced similarly to the American pronunciation, but are indeed, totally different. For example: "with"—the British dialect voices the [th] sound (like in the word [<u>th</u>is]), "privacy" becomes "<u>prih</u> vuh sih," "schedule" becomes "<u>sheh</u> jewuhl," "saint" becomes "snt" or "sn," "garage" becomes "<u>gare</u> azh" . . . and so forth. To be completely confident in the pronunciation of a British word, it is recommended that the actor invest in the English Pronouncing Dictionary by Daniel Jones. Also, a word and/or phrase-specific dictionary can be found online at:

    www.bbcamerica.com/content/141/dictionary

- The "Ask List" / ă → ah: One of the main errors made by American actors learning the British dialect is the overuse of the [ah] sound whenever a word is spelled with an [a]. The "ahsk list" seeks to eliminate that tendency by listing all of the words which substitute the [ah] sound instead of the [a] sound. If it is not on the list, use the "Bright ă" sound. For the complete "Ask List," see pages 81-83 of Lilene Mansell and Timothy Monich's book, *Speak with Distinction.* Or Google it.

pass, ask, answer, example → *pahs, ahsk, ahnsuh, exahmple*

ear → ih ~uh~:
The engineer cheered when the beer was cleared. We're fearful of nearly all weirdos.

air → eh ~uh~:
(note the "linking r" in the sentence below-notated with _____)
Where there is care, share the fare. She prepared her hair with care, don't stare!

oor → oo ~uh~:
(note the "linking r" in the sentence below-notated with _____)
I assure you the tour of Coors is for the mature. The poor pure boor is hard to endure.

ore → oh ~uh~ (very rounded):
The door was shorter than before the war. The Lord of Ford courted forty short girls.

are → ah:
(note the "linking r" in the sentence below-notated with _____)
Park your car and start your heart. The part of the art was hard to cart.

er → eh/uh:
Thirty thirsty servants were rehearsing the world's worst version of "Vertigo."

Intrusive "R":
California is where China is sending her. The idea of law is order and peace.

oh → ~uh~ oh:
Don't go to the road show, it's slow. Joe and Rose know the flow of the crow.

ah → or (very rounded):
The auditors called all the tawny blondes to the hall. She fawned all over Paul.

ah → o (rounded and popped):
The h*o*t c*o*pper c*o*ffee p*o*ts p*o*pped their t*o*ps. N*o*t in the p*o*t, C*o*lin!

ow → ah oo:
H*ow* n*ow* br*ow*n c*ow*? R*ou*nd and r*ou*nd with*ou*t a s*ou*nd, they f*ou*nd the gr*ou*nd.

Bright ă:
The c*a*t c*a*rried the *a*rrow to H*a*rry. *A*nne is in P*a*ris *a*cting *a*ngry at the p*a*rish.

Liquid U:
T*u*esday, the D*u*ke and the t*u*tor played n*ew* t*u*nes on the t*u*ba for the T*u*dors.

Prefixes/ Suffixes:
The _re_hearsal was _be_lieved to be _pre_paring the _de_livery of _de_light. I want_ed_ this.

Ask List/ ă → ah:
The st*a*ff at the c*a*stle thought the m*a*ster d*a*ft as he d*a*nced on the gr*a*ss near the b*a*ths.

STANDARD BRITISH DIALECT FILM/VIDEO/AUDIO
REFERENCES

INTERNET:
Internet sources can evolve and change over the years, so if any of the links below have expired, simply "Google search" the title of the link and you will be redirected to the updated site/location.

International Dialects of English Archive—www/dialectarchive. com
Speech Accent Archive—http://accent.gmu.edu/
BBC Voices Project—www.bbc.co.uk/voices/recordings
London's Voices—http://www.museumoflondon.org.uk/archive/ londonsvoices/

YOUTUBE:
TedTalks – *Patsy Rodenburg "Why I Do Theater"*
http://www.ted.com/talks/lang/eng/patsy_rodenburg_why_i_do_ theater.html

FILM/TV:

Downton Abbey (PBS)	Cast
The King's Speech	Cast
Harry Potter and . . . (all of them)	Cast
Chronicles of Narnia (all of them)	Cast
Pride & Prejudice	Cast
Sense & Sensibility	Cast
Gosford Park	Cast
Mansfield Park	Cast
Four Weddings and a Funeral, Notting Hill	Hugh Grant
The Sound of Music, Mary Poppins,	
Victor/Victoria, Thoroughly Modern Millie	Julie Andrews
Hamlet (Film and CD)	Kenneth Branagh's version
Shakespeare in Love	Dame Judi Dench, Joseph Fiennes, Gwyneth Paltrow
A Room With a View,	
Howard's End, Remains of the Day	Cast
("Merchant-Ivory" films*)*	

CD's/Coaches:
Standard British   Gillian Lane-Plescia
Stage Dialects   Jerry Blunt

For a more complete and detailed list of films/resources and a way to apply your knowledge to a role, see Ginny Kopf's book: *The Dialect Handbook*

BRITISH MONOLOGUES

FEMALE

AFTER MISS JULIE

Patrick Marber

BRITISH
MONOLOGUE
1 F

THE PLAY:

An "homage" to and adaptation of Strindberg's masterpiece, *Miss Julie*, Marber sets the classic tale in the British country-side post-World War II. Julie is the lady of the house—lonely, powerful and powerless at the same time. John is the chauffeur to Julie's father. Christine is John's lover and the cook on the estate. On the Midsummer Eve when the Labour Party wins its landslide victory in the elections, Julie joins the servants in the celebration and passions fly. Her "fall" from the heights of her position serves as the catalyst for the eventual tragedy at the end of the play.

The Monologue:

It is "the morning after" the Midsummer's Eve party/Labour Party celebrations and revelry on Miss Julie's estate. Julie (20's) tries to regain her composure and status in front of John.

TIME & PLACE:

The kitchen of a large country estate in England. Morning. June, 1945.

JULIE: Shut up! Have you seen the one with . . . I've lost my thought . . . did I tell you about my mother? She had this thing about women's emancipation . . . she swore she'd never marry so she told my father she would be his lover but never his wife.

Pause

But then . . . I was born. I was . . . a mistake, really.

[John: You're illegitimate?]

Mmm, funny isn't it? So they had to get married and my mother brought me up as . . . a child of nature. She wanted me to demonstrate the equality of the sexes. She used to dress me up in boy's clothes and made me learn about farming—she made me kill a fox when I was . . .

She pauses briefly, remembering

And then she reorganized the estate, the women had to do the men's work and the men the women's. We were the laughing stock of the whole county. Finally, my father snapped and she fell into line. But she began to stay out all night . . . she took lovers, people talked, she blamed my father for the failure of her experiment . . . her infidelities were her revenge. They rowed constantly, and fought, she often had terrible gashes and bruises . . . he did too, she was very strong when she was angry . . . and then there was a rumor that my father tried to kill himself . . .

John is stunned

Yes, he failed . . . *(smiles)* obviously.

Pause

I didn't know whose side I was on . . . I think I learnt all my emotions by the age of ten and never developed any more. A child experiences the world so deeply . . . without the sophistication to protect itself . . . it's not fair really.

Pause

My mother—almost on her deathbed—no, *on* her deathbed, made me swear that I'd never be a slave to any man.

BRITISH
MONOLOGUE
1 F

THE PLAY:

A brilliant device, Amy Freed takes modern sayings and incorporates them into "Old English" phrases seamlessly as she gives us another theory as to who *really* wrote Shakespeare's plays. Set in Elizabethan England and using the actual names of the people, players and aristocracy of the times, we follow the journey of a lowly farmer who seeks his fame and fortune with the Queen's Players in London. Under the protection of the "actual" writer, the 17th Earl of Oxford, Will Shakspere [sic —playwright's device] becomes the Player's playwright and provides the world with the stories and sonnets we've all come to know and love. But were they really *his*?

THE MONOLOGUE:

Anne (thirties) disguised herself as a "saucy wench" in order to blend in with the London city-folks and to spy on her husband. What she experienced as the saucy wench was a passionate love affair with her own husband! He was completely unaware of her true identity! Later, she falls prey to the charming Earl of Oxford. After their tryst, she walks back home to Stratford with the memories and revelations of her journey in London.

TIME & PLACE:

Elizabethan England. The road to Stratford. Dawn.

ANNE: What have I done! My ancient weakness loses me the day! I'm just a maid who can't say "nay." But neither could I well pronounce "decease," "desist," or "halt!." So now they bond, and I'm back out on the highway! I will back to Stratford, to cool my heals and hide my shame. At least let him still burn for her, which is, of course, myself. I was to have been revealed! He was to have discovered his wife in his slut and so LOVED me. But now he will discover a slut in his wife and then KILL me. As long as he thinks me ONLY a whore, he will continue to adore! I am SICK of men's philosophies. Of this mis-fired adventure, what am I to say—!!

(She takes Oxford's ring, now on a ribbon around her neck. Looks at it, for a moment. A slow burn, then a slow smile.)

That I had a wicked and sweet night once—that show'd me what life might be, if only I had not been me.

BRITISH
MONOLOGUE
1 F

THE PLAY:

Is she a ghost? Is she the future? Is she the past?

Kandi has some sort of an angel hanging around her, freezing scenes in her life, rewinding them, helping Kandi change her choices before she ruins her life. In flashbacks, we see that Stacey *was* Kandi and if someone had been *her* angel, her life might have turned out much different. But then, would there have ever even *been* a "Kandi"?

THE MONOLOGUE:

In this flashback scene, Stacey (teens) confronts her soon-to-be stepfather in the booth of a local disco club where young kids use fake i.d.'s to get in and party.

TIME & PLACE:

A local club. Day time. The present. England.

STACEY: *(to John)* OK. I'll make you a deal. You might do this one.

(she edges closer to him)

I'm going to tell you something. When I've told you, I'm going to go away and never come back. And you're going to go home and tell my Mum that I'm fine and I'll be in touch. I think I'll have the flu on the wedding day, but I'll send a card. I'll call her when I can and you'll make her see that it's for the best.

(moves ever closer)

Because if you don't, I'll go into school tomorrow and tell the head that when you and me were seen in here tonight, you tried it on with me and I mean *seen.*

(he follows her gaze)

Yeh, they're all from year 11. In fact, they're in your class. See . . . you always thought I never listen to you, but you said to me, if you're smart, you'll tell the head it was Mrs. G's fault. And I said, who'd believe me? And you said: everyone. Remember?

(she pushes him away, gently. He's in shock)

BRITISH
MONOLOGUE
1 F

THE PLAY:

Charlie Silver deals with the loss of her brother in a motorcycle accident by trying to live his life for him. She tries to become the biggest troublemaker in school, she collects a "gang" of boys to ride the same motorcycle street-race route that her brother rode, and all the while she tries to suppress her natural musical talent. She almost manages to maintain this hard façade until a special music teacher breaks through and discovers Charlie's true talent.

THE MONOLOGUE:

Miss Fry (thirties) has succeeded in getting Charlie to buckle down and learn the craft of piano. Here, she remembers her own first "gig" as a musician and what the playing of music can do for one's soul.

TIME & PLACE:

Present. The stage at school. After school. England.

MISS FRY: It's pretty bad. Sometimes you're up onstage and you're counting the bars in your head, when you shouldn't . . . because it should be like breathing . . . I shouldn't be telling you this Charlie, it will make you more nervous about your exam.

[Charlie: It won't]

My first gig was at a place called Running Horse. Total dive. The back of beyond, one crappy listing in the local paper, the place where old men with no teeth go to die. You psyche yourself up to imagine that this is your crowning moment, this is where it all comes together, life starts to get perfect. The stage was a bit like a pen, you feel like you're about to be pelted with broken bottles or cabbages.

[Charlie: No way!]

But it didn't matter because I was with my first band and it was the first time we'd had an audience. And it was kind of blessed, as a lot of first times are. It becomes more than a gig, it becomes everything. But this was always in the air, this first performance. Even when we were just sitting around after rehearsals having a drink and a laugh, we carried it with us in our mind's eye. How we would look and how the guitars caught the light and how you saved yourself for your little moment, not for what people would say when they looked at you, but for how you wouldn't be there anymore. You might catch someone's eye, you might be singing to the leg of a chair at the back of the room, just seeing the varnish, the sheen of it, but you don't *know*. This was the thing with the music. You did it because you wanted to become backdrop, even to yourself. You wanted to make yourself vanish.

(pause)

Come on. Your piece, your exam. (beat) Once more, and with feeling.

Suzy Almond

BRITISH
MONOLOGUE
1 F

THE PLAY:

Charlie Silver deals with the loss of her brother in a motorcycle accident by trying to live his life for him. She tries to become the biggest troublemaker in school, she collects a "gang" of boys to ride the same motorcycle street-race route that her brother rode, and all the while she tries to suppress her natural musical talent. She almost manages to maintain this hard façade until a special music teacher breaks through and discovers Charlie's true talent.

THE MONOLOGUE:

Practicing for her piano certificate, Charlie completely forgot to show up to the motorcycle challenge. Was it a mistake? Or was it a blessing to have this new focus as an excuse to miss the race because the motorcycle she promised them wasn't nearly ready to be ridden again? Charlie (fifteen) attempts to explain her new focus in life to a very angry Lee (fifteen) when he confronts her about missing the motorcycle race she had promised they would win.

TIME & PLACE:

Present. The stage at school. Half an hour after the motorcycle race. England.

CHARLIE: *(to Lee)* She . . . . One lesson . . . you see, some lessons she didn't actually teach. And sometimes, especially at the beginning, what she did was boring, you don't wanna hear, she drones. But now and again . . . One time she was about to play a song about a lady who drowned in a river, but it was nothing to do with the lesson, it was just that she liked it. I said, it sounds miserable to me, Miss. But she said hang on, and she told me the story: it's a sad song, she said . . . she fought for love and she lost . . . and now her skin is white as lily, her lips are rose red, she's still, and she floats downstream. She told me to close my eyes and imagine it was a dark moonlit night and that the water was lapping around the lady, taking her in. She said that when she got to the bridge of the song, there would be a special note that didn't sound like the rest of the tune. It was a high sound, extra sad, a black key near the end of the piano and when I heard it I had to imagine it was like a shooting star bursting across the river, trying to wake up the lady. I told her I couldn't be bothered, but when she started to play . . . And at the end of the second verse, when she hit that key and the sound broke, I felt the note shoot through the roof of this room like a bullet and I saw the star burst and I wanted the lady to wake up. I couldn't wait for that note to come round again. So that she'd open her eyes.

BRITISH
MONOLOGUE
1 F

THE PLAY:

The sweeping and beautiful romantic saga of the Dashwood sisters is a classic tale of love, heroism, betrayal and loyalty. After their father dies, the home and lifestyle they knew is handed down to their elder half-brother and natural heir to their father's estate. Widows and female children were not given access to the family fortune unless through the kindness of any male relatives. Marriage and romance was not just a passing fancy, but often a fiscal and physical necessity. The two eldest daughters could not be more different in their personalities and affections. Elinor, the eldest, is sensible and "unromantic"—at least on the surface. Marianne, her younger sister, has more of the open-spirited, passionate sensibility. These two qualities draw two decidedly different suiters to each woman, and what follows is a story of heartbreak, silent suffering, and ultimate happiness for both of them.

THE MONOLOGUE:

Edward has been visiting his sister (the Dashwood heir's wife) at the Dashwood's Norland Park estate. He has endeared himself to the Dashwood sisters immediately—but seems especially connected to Elinor. As their romance seems certain and a proposal all but imminent, Mrs. Dashwood asks Marianne (sixteen) her opinion of her potential brother-in-law.

TIME & PLACE:

The sitting room. Norland Park, Sussex, England. Late 1700's.

MARIANNE: Edward is very amiable, and I love him tenderly. But yet—he is not the kind of young man—there is a something wanting—his figure is not striking; it has none of that grace which I should expect in the man who could seriously attach my sister. His eyes do not have that spirit, that fire, which all together show his virtue and intelligence. And, besides all this, I am afraid, mama, he has no real taste. Music seems scarcely interesting to him, and though he admires Elinor's drawings very much, he does not admire them as a person who can understand their worth. It is evident, in spite of his frequent attention to her while she draws, that in fact he knows nothing of the matter. He admires as a lover, not as a connoisseur.

To satisfy me, those characters must be united. I could not be happy with a man whose taste did not in every point coincide with mine. He must share all my feelings; the same books, the same music must charm us both.

Oh! mama, how spiritless, how tame was Edward's manner in reading to us last night! I felt so awful for my sister. Yet, she was so composed, she seemed to scarcely notice his deficiency. I could hardly keep my seat. To hear those beautiful lines which have frequently almost driven me wild, pronounced with such impenetrable calmness, such dreadful indifference! Elinor has not my feelings, and therefore she may overlook it and be happy with him. But it would have broke *my* heart had I loved him, to hear him read with so little sensibility.

Mama, the more I know of the world, the more I am convinced I shall never see a man whom I can really love. I require so much!

BRITISH
MONOLOGUE
1 F

THE PLAY:

The sweeping and beautiful romantic saga of the Dashwood sisters is a classic tale of love, heroism, betrayal and loyalty. After their father dies, the home and lifestyle they knew is handed down to their elder half-brother and natural heir to their father's estate. Widows and female children were not given access to the family fortune unless through the kindness of any male relatives. Marriage and romance was not just a passing fancy, but often a fiscal and physical necessity. The two eldest daughters could not be more different in their personalities and affections. Elinor, the eldest, is sensible and "unromantic"—at least on the surface. Marianne, her younger sister, has more of the open-spirited, passionate sensibility. These two qualities draw two decidedly different suiters to each woman, and what follows is a story of heartbreak, silent suffering, and ultimate happiness for both of them.

THE MONOLOGUE:

Edward has been visiting his sister (the Dashwood heir's wife) at the Dashwood's Norland Park estate. He has endeared himself to the Dashwood sisters immediately—but seems especially connected to Elinor. As their romance seems certain and a proposal all but imminent, Marianne asks for confirmation from Elinor that she is, indeed, going to be engaged to Edward. Elinor (nineteen) is not willing to commit to feelings that may not be returned and since there is no firm engagement as yet, she remains optimistic but realistic . . . or, sensible.

TIME & PLACE:

Elinor's room. Norland Park, Sussex, England. Late 1700's.

ELINOR: I do not attempt to deny that I think very highly of him—that I greatly esteem, that I like him. Excuse me, and be assured that I meant no offense to you, by speaking, in so quiet a way, of my own feelings. Believe them to be stronger than I have declared; believed them, in short to be such as his merit. But farther than this you must not believe. I am by no means assured of his regard for me. There are moments when the extent of it seems doubtful; and till his sentiments are fully known you cannot wonder at my wishing to avoid any encouraging of my own feelings for him by believing or calling it more than it is. In my heart I feel little—scarcely *any* doubt of his preference. But there are other points to be considered besides his inclination. He is very far from being independent. What his mother really is we cannot know; and I am very much mistaken if Edward is not himself aware that there would be many difficulties in his way, if he were to wish to marry a woman who had neither a great fortune nor high rank.

BRITISH
MONOLOGUE
1 F

THE PLAY:

A journey-through-time sort of play that weaves the past, present and future all together in an evocative, theatrical, haunting tapestry that leaves the audience stunned at the surprising twists and turns. The play takes place between 1959 and 2039. We see vignettes of the relationships of five "couples"—Henry and Elizabeth (man and wife), Elizabeth and Gabriel (mother and son), Gabriel & Gabrielle (lovers), Gabrielle & John (husband and wife) and Gabriel II and Andrew (father and son)—and how their lives are wonderfully and frightfully intertwined.

THE MONOLOGUE:

Elizabeth (thirties) has just been visited by the police in regards to the behavior of her husband at a public park. Throughout their time together, there have been clues to his "tendencies," but nothing as concrete as her discovery today. As she sets Henry free and does not turn him in to the authorities she says to him "you have stolen the future"—a poignant statement which comes near the end of the play as we have seen how her decision to let him leave played out in the lives of their son's and grandson's lives.

TIME & PLACE:

Henry and Elizabeth's flat. London. 1968. Night time. A stormy day.

ELIZABETH: Well, that's what I thought. I thought my mind is running away. Clearly, I was going mad. And that's what I told them, of course. There's been some misunderstanding. I know my husband. He doesn't interfere with children. He has a son of his own. He's a father. Nevertheless, they said, they still want to speak to you. That's what I said. I said this is not right. How dare you accuse my husband of such a thing. Against nature. And I sent them on their way, Henry. I showed them the door. I could not have been more indignant. And when they were gone and I was alone, it felt to me as if the world had been turned upside down. And I looked around and saw just how dirty our room was. Filthy, in fact. In the corners and on the windowsills and the ceilings. Layers of dust and dirt and grime and dead insects. Years of neglect, Henry. How did we let it come to this? And so I began to clean it. A bucket of hot water and soap suds. I washed the walls, the ceilings, even the light fittings were scrubbed. I washed the door handles and the light switches and the dark corners behind the furniture. I scrubbed the table and the floor and polished the windows. I dusted the books and the lampshade and even took to the grouting between the tiles with a toothbrush. And when I finished I looked around and it looked exactly the same. So I found an old tin of leftover paint in the cupboard. And as the tanks rolled into Prague, I painted. And I painted. And I painted. Then I hung the pictures back on the walls. And put the books back on the bookshelves and moved the furniture back into position and it was when I was moving the wardrobe that it tilted slightly and something slipped from the top . . . and landed at my feet,

>*(beat)*

a leather satchel. Quite old. Quite worn. Good—quality leather. Something you have had since you were a child. Given to you by an uncle, you once said. And inside there is a collection of photographs of young children, boys mainly, naked, some involved in sexual acts with adults. Some of them clearly distressed. Clearly frightened. And among the photographs. Among the photographs, Henry, are pictures of our own son.

>*(silence)*

Have you touched him?

BRITISH MONOLOGUES

MALE

BRITISH
MONOLOGUE
1 M

THE PLAY:

In the theater world of London in the 1630's, all the female roles were played by boys. They were usually orphans who were "adopted" (bought) by owner/managers of theater companies and they could be "apprenticed" (sold) to anyone else at will. Using real people as sources, Nicholas Wright gives us a glimpse into the complex emotional, moral, and financial lives of a group of players and their owner/teacher, John Shank, as he struggles with heavy debt and the arrival of a new boy.

THE MONOLOGUE:

Stephen (fourteen), a boy actor, shares his story of how he entered the world of acting as he attempts to bond with his mentor/teacher/owner.

TIME & PLACE:

London. 1630's. Shank's house, evening.

STEPHEN: I dressed up once. Although I wouldn't exactly call it acting. It was last Easter weekend. I'd taken down some curtains in the Dining-room. And I'd wrapped them round me. And I was standing on the table when my father walked in. And the very next week, he and my mother brought me down to London. They signed me up with a draper and I thought, 'oh good, they like me after all.' But when I went back to where we were staying, to say good-bye, they'd gone. They'd paid the bill and left me a pair of shoes. I thought they'd both gone mad. They never wrote. And then one night, I met a tinker. He'd been to Hellefield. He'd actually mended their pots and pans. He said that all the time he was tapping away, they were laughing and holding hands. He said they looked as though they'd just got married.

CRESSIDA

Nicholas Wright

BRITISH
MONOLOGUE
1 M

THE PLAY:

In the theater world of London in the 1630's, all the female roles were played by boys. They were usually orphans who were "adopted" (bought) by owner/managers of theater companies and they could be "apprenticed" (sold) to anyone else at will. Using real people as sources, Nicholas Wright gives us a glimpse into the complex emotional, moral, and financial lives of a group of players and their owner/teacher, John Shank, as he struggles with heavy debt and the arrival of a new boy.

THE MONOLOGUE:

Stephen (fourteen)—the newest boy actor—and his idol, Honey have snuck into the competitor's theater to steal costumes in order to pay off their manager's debt. After almost being caught, they come up from their hiding place to discover that the gowns they were going to steal are now gone.

TIME & PLACE:

1630's. London. The costume-store (storage room) of the competitor's theater. Dark of night.

[Honey: Shanky will have to sell you after all.]

STEPHEN: He won't. Do you really not know what I did today? Did you honestly think that Master Gunnell had sent me with a message? Or that he'd promised me First Fairy? Of course he hadn't. I made it up. I made it all up. I couldn't believe that you all believed me.

   (pause)

I woke up this morning. And the house was empty. And I remembered it was Tuesday, and that Master Shank would need his Fairies. And everything fitted. Because all I wanted, was to be where you were. Right from the very first time I saw you act. I wanted to talk with you. And smoke, just like we did tonight. I wanted to ask you, why did Samuel lock me in the cupboard? Why am I funny? Why are people always getting rid of me?

   (pause)

And now that I've got you, I won't be got rid of again. I won't allow it.

British
Monologue
1 M

The Play:

As a family gathers together to mourn the sudden loss of their father and to try and make sense of his unexpected suicide, the former-British citizens, now Americans, find solace and common ground in their disdain for their adopted country.

The Monologue:

Paul (thirty-two) responds to the "anti-American" banter with his own impressions of foreigners.

Time & Place:

A home in New England—outside the City. The kitchen. After dinner (bad Chinese food). Evening.

PAUL: The funny thing about living in America as a foreigner is the way you see other foreigners act. They love to criticize. Everything's—what? Rubbish? Some things are and some things aren't. That's how I see things, but . . . I had a friend from London visiting with us—to him everything was either stupid or plastic or barbaric. Then you couldn't get him out of the damn sun. At night you couldn't get him away from the damn TV. (*he sips his water*) But I know why this is. I've thought about this a lot. It's all so—threatening. It's too much for some people to handle. The size of everything. The importance of everything. So they're actually being defensive. They're scared.

> (*beat*)

I hate having friends from home visit now. It's so predictable.

To answer your question: I have read a couple of nice scripts this week. We'll see. I've been reading long enough to know that you can never know. You do your best. And try to have an impact where you can. (*he sips his water*) The other day, I had a thought. You get these kinds of thoughts reading scripts. Let's say there are maybe 10,000 film scripts in circulation in L.A. on any given day. I think I'm being conservative. And each script will have at least 20 copies. Probably more, but let's say 20. And each script—the rule is about 110 pages. That's—. I did the math before, something like twenty-two million pages of film script just—on any given day.

> (*beat*)

Now if each writer were to say just indent—both left and right margins—by say three spaces less. Three spaces—no more. It would mean each script would be about five pages shorter—or a total savings of about one million pages, which I'm told roughly equals 200 trees.

> (*short pause*)

I wrote a memo. (*shrugs*) Who knows?

A NUMBER

Caryl Churchill

BRITISH
MONOLOGUE
1M

THE PLAY:

A dynamic study of "what-if"—exploring the controversial topic of human cloning, Churchill leads us on a journey of twists and turns that leaves us questioning the benefits of cloning. Nothing is truly resolved and we are left wondering if it's worth it at all.

THE MONOLOGUE:

"B2" (Bernard–age thirty-five) is the second of Salter's "sons."He was his father's "do-over."After his genetic mother killed herself and his genetic cloned brother was sent to foster care, his father waited for him (B2) to come. As Salter waited, he stopped drinking and became a better man—better than he was to his first son (B1). B2 has just found out that there are "others" out there, and he and his genetic father discuss "nature" and "nurture."*(Note: the rhythm of the speech in this piece is to be interpreted personally by the actor. No punctuation clues are provided for your breathing/pausing cues, so try it many different ways to find the right fit)*

TIME & PLACE:

"Where Salter lives."The present.

B2: Maybe he shouldn't blame you, maybe it was a genetic, could you help drinking we don't know or drugs at the time philosophically as I understand it it wasn't viewed as not like now when our understanding's different and would a different person genetically different person not have been so been so vulnerable because there could always be some genetic addictive and then again someone with the same genetic exactly the same but at a different time a different cultural and of course all the personal all kinds of what happened in your own life your childhood or things all kind of because suppose you'd had a brother with identical an identical twin say but separated at birth so you had entirely different early you see what I'm saying would he have done the same things who can say he might have been a very loving father and in fact of course you have that in you to be that because you were to me so it's a combination of very complicated and that's who you were so probably I shouldn't blame you.

BRITISH
MONOLOGUE
1 M

THE PLAY:

Charlie Silver deals with the loss of her brother in a motorcycle accident by trying to live his life for him. She tries to become the biggest troublemaker in school, she collects a "gang" of boys to ride the same motorcycle street-race route that her brother rode, and all the while she tries to suppress her natural musical talent. She almost manages to maintain this hard façade until a special music teacher breaks through and discovers Charlie's true talent.

THE MONOLOGUE:

Paul (fifteen) and Charlie (fifteen) are trying to outdo each other in a contest of sorts. Each one is trying to cause the teachers in their school to have a nervous breakdown. Who can get thrown out of class the quickest? Who can create the most havoc? Who can bring a teacher to tears? After a failed attempt to set off firecrackers in class, Paul tries to redeem his reputation by recounting one of his *successful* pranks.

NOTE: The dialect of this piece/play can venture towards a more Cockney/Estuary English sound as is evidenced by the syntax written into the rhythm of the speakers.

TIME & PLACE:

Present. A school hall. England.

PAUL: Yesterday, I got inside McGivney's head after fifteen seconds of coming into class, I think you'll find. Just sitting down, everyone's going "Go on then, Paul." I goes "Sir" and I've got this Muller yogurt blob on Dwayne's ruler and it's strawberry and it's poised and *everyone* is thinking—*no way*. Cos it's McGivney. But I think you'll find that I don't care. He turns round and I goes "Happy Birthday Sir"—it's not even his birthday—it just made it more funnier—and I pulled back the end of the ruler—I pulled it back with *skill*—it was *skillful*, and I let it go. Slow motion pink blob leaving launch pad now. Splat on McGivney's snooker glasses what are too big for his face. He makes this squeaking noise like a hamster, I goes to *everyone* "he sounds like a hamster." He goes "Paul Gibbs!" I goes "What?" I should of took a stop watch. Fifteen seconds! I've got witnesses.

BRITISH
MONOLOGUE
1 M

THE PLAY:

Charlie Silver deals with the loss of her brother in a motorcycle accident by trying to live his life for him. She tries to become the biggest troublemaker in school, she collects a "gang" of boys to ride the same motorcycle street-race route that her brother rode, and all the while she tries to suppress her natural musical talent. She almost manages to maintain this hard façade until a special music teacher breaks through and discovers Charlie's true talent.

THE MONOLOGUE:

Lee (fifteen) and Paul (fifteen) are hanging out at the car park listening to music and waiting for Charlie to arrive with her motorcycle. Though they both are enjoying the same song and the same band, they like it for different reasons, as Lee tries to illuminate for Paul.

TIME & PLACE:

Present. Early evening. Dark. A car park. England.

LEE: I've been to see them.

   [Paul: But it was cold out, yeh, sold out.]

They came out of nothing so they mean something. They could have ended up working for the Drain Doctor—playing with sink plungers all day, picking up twenty pence tips from old ladies. But no, they're making music, *no-one's* calling them stupid. Music for the street, from the street . . . battle rhymes, songs about blood and tears and fat tunes that come up through your feet and won't leave you alone. Everything you were thinking, it's like they stole it from your head when you were sleeping. You wake up and they're playing *your* song on the radio. You wake up and say how did you *know* that, man? And if some girl, or some kid in a car park said those words to me and there was no beat, no tune, what would I do? I would laugh in their face. But these guys . . . I mean, they could of been Drain Doctors.

BRITISH
MONOLOGUE
1 M

THE PLAY:

A journey-through-time sort of play that weaves the past, present and future all together in an evocative, theatrical, haunting tapestry that leaves the audience stunned at the surprising twists and turns. The play takes place between 1959 and 2039. We see vignettes of the relationships of five "couples"— Henry and Elizabeth (man and wife), Elizabeth and Gabriel (mother and son), Gabriel & Gabrielle (lovers), Gabrielle & John (husband and wife) and Gabriel II and Andrew (father and son)—and how their lives are wonderfully and frightfully intertwined.

THE SCENE:

Gabriel (twenty-eight) visits with his mother (Elizabeth) who has been carrying around a hideous secret for most of Gabriel's life. Again, Gabriel seeks to find out the truth about his father. Where is he? Why did he leave us? His mother will not budge in her refusal to discuss the man (Henry) who abandoned them when Gabriel was just seven years old.

TIME & PLACE:

Elizabeth's flat. London. 1988. Dinner time.

GABRIEL: (*to his mother*) I used to collect stamps. Do you remember? I have stamps from all over the world, from countries that don't even exist anymore, all neatly laid out in albums. A different album for every country and three of every stamp. One to keep, one to replace it in case it is damaged, and one to swap should the opportunity arise.

So I was searching through these stamp albums when I found a newspaper clipping tucked in the back of one of them. It was dated sometime in 1970. So I must have been, I don't know, ten, and I had forgotten about it of course, as you do. You forget these things. But it was a report about the disappearance of a man at Ayers Rock, in Australia. Do you remember it?

(*she is silent*)

A man was seen climbing the rock at dusk by campers. Several people passed him on the way down and warned him to turn back. It was getting dark. You're not allowed up there at night. It's dangerous. Easy to fall. But he wouldn't listen. He continued to climb . . . He was described as being a man of fair complexion with an English accent. Anyway, he failed to return. And despite an extensive search, no trace of him was ever found. (*beat*) I mean, I'm sure there's an explanation but I remember being taken by this all the same, wondering what happened to the man and whether somehow he was still up there, as though he had slipped into some kind of parallel time frame. You know how children's minds think.

It's funny the things you remember, but I remember searching through your sewing drawer for the good scissors which you hated me using to cut paper with. And I knew I shouldn't be doing it but children will always look where they're not meant to. And I found them. (*beat*) The scissors. And I cut out the article and tucked it into the back of this stamp album . . . And I must have forgotten about it, and there it was all these years later, and I found myself thinking about this man again, this fair-skinned Englishman and wondering who he was . . . and what happened to him.

BRITISH
MONOLOGUE
1 M

THE PLAY:

A journey-through-time sort of play that weaves the past, present and future all together in an evocative, theatrical, haunting tapestry that leaves the audience stunned at the surprising twists and turns. The play takes place between 1959 and 2039. We see vignettes of the relationships of five "couples"—Henry and Elizabeth (man and wife), Elizabeth and Gabriel (mother and son), Gabriel & Gabrielle (lovers), Gabrielle & John (husband and wife) and Gabriel II and Andrew (father and son)—and how their lives are wonderfully and frightfully intertwined.

THE SCENE:

Gabriel (twenty-eight) has traveled from London to Australia in the hopes of finding his father (Henry) who abandoned the family when Gabriel was just seven years old. Here, he reveals his reasons to the woman (Gabrielle) he just met at the small bed & breakfast she runs near The Coorong on the southern coast of Australia.

TIME & PLACE:

1988. Night. A beach. The Coorong. A storm on the horizon.

[Gabrielle: What about your father . . . do you remember him?]

GABRIEL: *(to his Gabrielle)* I wish I could say yes. I wish I could say that I remember the touch of his bristles on my face, or the scent of his aftershave, or the sound of his laughter in the morning. But I remember none of that. He's a mystery. What I remember is his absence and my mother's silence. All I have are his postcards. And they don't make much sense. They're full of wild predictions about the weather and the end of the world. In one he wrote that he had seen a vision of a fish falling from the sky and the earth being covered by water.

   [Gabrielle: Was he mad?]

I don't know . . . Perhaps. The last postcard he wrote was sent from Ayers Rock. It has a picture of the rock with storm clouds gathering. It is bright red. Unbelievably red. With these great purple clouds ready to burst above it. "Dear Son," he wrote, "In the desert, on a clear night, if you know where to look, you can see the planet Saturn. The word planet derives from the Greek and means wanderer. Saturn is named after the Roman god who devoured his own son. Forgive me. Your loving father, Henry Law. P.S. There's snow falling on the Rock tonight."

   [Gabrielle: It doesn't snow in the desert.]

No. And fish don't fall out of the sky. And fathers don't leave their children. And mothers don't drown themselves in the sea. *(beat)* So that's what I'm doing here.

In the past ten years of coaching the Irish dialect for the stage, a few common experiences have arisen. In each production, a very specific region of Ireland was studied and explored through sound. Whether it was Dublin, Donegal, Belfast, or Galway, every attempt at accuracy, specificity and colloquial truth was made . . . with varying degrees of success. Audiences for each of the shows responded with varying degrees of approval—"That was so dead-on" or "Were they supposed to be Irish?" or "What county was HE supposed to be from?" or "They sounded just like my brothers/mother/aunt," etc. In the same audience, members of the Irish community from the same county in Ireland would swear that the dialect they heard on stage that night was/was not from their county of origin! The long and short of it is: for every speaker of an Irish dialect, there is another speaker from the same region who may sound completely different, and the Irish in audience may not agree on who is right!

While frustrating to actors and coaches alike, the variety of sound choices that exist in modern speakers of the Irish dialect (both in Ireland and abroad) can offer a bit of comfort on some level. If your sound differs slightly from your co-actors, it can be justified as being truthful to the circumstances of your character. Each speaker has a different history. You may all have been raised in County Cork, but *your* father was Scottish and your mother was from Dublin, and so you will speak slightly differently than your Cork schoolmate. Justified.

Mind you, this is not a license to become *unspecific* in your sounds. On the contrary, you must know exactly what sounds do exist in your region in order to acquire or adapt them to your character's circumstances. In a play where the characters all originate from or inhabit the same area, we need to have the regional base from which others can diverge to create the real world sounds of the play. The proper nouns (names of people and places) in the play need to be pronounced the same by every member of the cast, but there can be some flexibility in the other words you may speak because of your character's background. If you are from Belfast, you would not sound as if you are from Cork. If you are from Dublin, you would take great pains to sound unlike anyone in the country (anyplace outside of Dublin). If you are from Cork, but then moved to Dublin, when you return to Cork, you would sound different than your neighbors and friends who never left Cork. And so on. Ultimately, you must do your research to discover the specific regional needs of your sound and work hard to achieve as close an approximation to the sound as you possibly can.

In the section that follows, sound changes are illuminated that represent some common sound changes in Hiberno-English (Irish) dialects. Two specific sections organize the sounds: "Dublin" and "Regional."Not all of them exist in any one region. When you research your specific region of the country, you can highlight the changes below that match the sounds you need to use for your character. The dialect changes for Northern Ireland (part of Great Britain) are not included. The changes discussed below exist in the Republic of Ireland.

MOUTH/PHYSICAL THOUGHTS:

● My teachers taught me that the physical conditions of an environment (cold, foggy, windy) can have a physical effect on the shape of your mouth, and therefore the sounds of your speech, when you talk. For example, in California (where I live), it is sunny and bright a great deal of the time. So are the people. We smile a lot! That "smile" has found its way into our speech patterns and our vowel sounds tend to come out all smiling . . . even the "round" ones. In fact, trying to teach California actors <u>not</u> to smile when they speak is a quite a challenge! In Ireland, the cold, damp air could have had an effect on the mouths of the Irish people. They tend to speak with very little mouth opening (to prevent the cold from coming in?) and a rounder, tighter lip position.

● Because of the tight mouth positions and the "hard R" sounds, your jaw and tongue will get very tense. Be sure to warm up your jaw before doing this dialect, as you may find yourself getting vocally tired very quickly.

● The "soft t" or "soft d" is sometimes spelled out in a script as "th" or "dh" . . . this simply means that you must put your tongue behind your top teeth to make this sound.

SOUND/MUSIC THOUGHTS:

● One of the first things an actor notices when studying the Irish dialect is the music of the dialect. We love music. We learn things musically (how many times have you been accused of saying your lines the same way over and over? You've learned them in a "musical" pattern!). The danger of doing that with the Irish dialect is that you will sound like a bad American television commercial or a cartoon leprechaun if you're not careful. There is some music in the dialect, but remember to *let the meaning of the line control the music, don't let the music control the meaning.*

Kimberly Mohne Hill   71

● The music of the dialect tends to be more present in heightened circumstances or storytelling moments. For example, if you were to tell your parents about an incident that happened to you at school that really affected you, your voice would become more animated and energized. The same is true for the strength of the Irish dialect. When they are "narrating" a story, they color it with all the vocal colors they can. The music plays in their voices.

● Because the Irish use so many quotations, proverbs and clichés in their everyday speech, they tend to speak faster than the average person. Onstage, the pace of utterance may be too strong for the audience's understanding. Though it may be accurate to be fast, it may not be effective.

● More noticeably than with the English accents, the Irish have colloquialisms that are more rhythmically written in to their literature. Usually these phrases, words or interjections are not to be taken literally, but poetically as part of the natural rhythm of the line. For example, "Sure, it's not too hot in here is it?" The word "sure" is the interjection/toss off word.

● When the Irish do pause to compose a thought, the "nonverbal" interjection they often use instead of our American "um" is "am."

Irish Dialect Sound Changes

Consonant Changes:

Throughout Ireland—

The Question of "R"—use the hard (American) "r" sound for all diphthongs and vowels of "r"
Here is their poor horse cart. Sir, it's your mother.

[ing] → *[in] going, coming, doing* → *goin', comin', doin'*

[t] in final position *bet, wet, hit, kite* → *bet$_h$, wet$_h$, hit$_h$, kit$_h$*
(Lots of air)

[th] → *[t$_h$] cathedrals, thanks, theater* → *cat$_h$edrals, t$_h$anks, t$_h$eater*
(Using your tongue behind your top teeth, try to make the actual [th] sound as written, just don't stick your tongue out. It may come out sounding a bit like [th])

[th] → *[d$_h$] this, them, those, weather* → *d$_h$is, d$_h$em, d$_h$ose, wea d$_h$er*
(Using your tongue behind your top teeth, try to make the actual [th] sound as written, just don't stick your tongue out. It may come out sounding a bit like [dh])

[t/d] → *[t$_h$/d$_h$] drink, what, write* → *d$_h$rink, what$_h$, wroyt$_h$*
(The consonant [t] and [d] sounds are dentalized (meaning your tongue is touching the back of your top teeth) and lots of air falls off of those sounds. Just think of the [h] symbol as a clue to have a bit more air come out after you make the consonant sound.)

Vowel Changes:

Most Common/Dublin—

[a] → *[a] grand, fan, class, pat, palm, man, sandwich*
(Becomes not as crisp as the Bright ă sound. Round your lips and say "ah" and then smile to make this sound in words like "grand," "Pat," "calm," etc.)
[uh] → *[oo] mother, Dublin, love,* → *moother, Dooblin, loov,*
(The schwa sound becomes more like the [u] sound as in the word "put" or "took")

Kimberly Mohne Hill   73

[ow] → [uh-oo]   mouth, out, South   →   muh-ooth, uh-oot,

[oh] → [_{uh}ou]   go, show, slow,   →   g_{uh}ou, sh_{uh}ou, sl_{uh}ou
(A short schwa glide into the "oh" sound with a little bit of tightening - Dublin)

[aw] → [ah /aw]   ought, all, straw   →   aht, ahl, straw

[o] → [o: / ah]   not, God, pot   →   naht, Go:d, paht

[ay] → [_{uh}ei]   take, name, face, days   →   t_{uh}eik, n_{uh}eim, f_{uh}eis, d_{uh}eiz
(A short schwa glide into the "ay" sound with a little bit of tightening - Dublin)

COMMON IN REGIONS–
(IN ADDITION TO SOME OF THE SOUNDS ABOVE)

[oh] → [o:]   go, show, slow, road   →   goh:, sh oh:, sl oh:, r o:d
(Lengthened and tightened in others areas of Ireland. No diphthong.)

[ay] → [e:]   space, blame, date   →   speh:s, bleh:m, deh:t
(Lengthened and tightened in others areas of Ireland. No diphthong.)

[oo] → [_{uh} oo] school, new, student   →   sch_{uh}ool, n_{uh}oo, st_{uh}oodent

[eye] → [uh ee/oy]   find, try, crime   →   fuh eend, troy, cruh eem,

[ih] → [eh]   fifty, into, give, skin   →   fefty, ento, gev, sken

Hard [r]
The horse cart was there at the start. Serve the Colonel the first course.

[ing] → [in]
They were coming and going while watching the racing. Walking is better than running.

Final [tʰ]
I bet when it's wet you'll hit the bar. That fellow will just strut up to the front!

[th] → [tʰ/dʰ]
Thanks for the thought, but no thanks. I think the theater is through with them.

[t/d] → [tʰ/dʰ]
You'd better not drink that water. Don't drink drunk. Take that tired talk home.

[a] → [a]
That man has a handsome manner. Be calm, the fans at the castle will scramble.

[uh] → [oo]
Me mother and me brother went to London for the summer. One day someone will come

[ow] → [uh-oo]
Now the sound of the loud crowd fills the town. The crown fell down on the ground.

[aw] → [ah/aw]
All the tall daughters called for Paul. I caught a cold on the walk to the mall.

[o] → [o: or ah]
Not the hot pot of tea! Honestly, you need to stop watching those cop shows.

[oh] → [ᵤₕou/o:]
Go sl<u>ow</u> near the sh<u>ow</u> by the r<u>oa</u>d, J<u>oe</u>. D<u>o</u>n't sh<u>ow</u> R<u>o</u>se the n<u>o</u>te from the h<u>o</u>st.

[ay] → [ᵤₕei/e:]
You can t<u>a</u>ke me n<u>a</u>me but you can't t<u>a</u>ke me f<u>a</u>ce. It's gr<u>ea</u>t to pl<u>ay</u> in the h<u>ay</u> with K<u>a</u>te.

[oo] → [ᵤₕ oo]
The n<u>ew</u> sch<u>oo</u>l r<u>u</u>les were cr<u>ue</u>l to the st<u>u</u>dents. Sh<u>oo</u>t, it's a gr<u>ue</u>ling f<u>eu</u>d.

[eye] → [uh ee/oy]
<u>I</u>reland at n<u>i</u>ght is s<u>i</u>lent and k<u>i</u>nd of fr<u>i</u>ghtening. The f<u>i</u>ne p<u>i</u>ne tree was m<u>i</u>ne.

[ih] → [eh]
G<u>i</u>ve a d<u>i</u>fferent g<u>i</u>ft to the gu<u>i</u>ld members. The m<u>i</u>tt <u>i</u>s <u>i</u>n the k<u>i</u>tchen, F<u>i</u>nn.

INTERNET SOURCES:

Internet sources can evolve and change over the years, so if any of the links below have expired, simply "Google search" the title of the link and you will be redirected to the updated site/location.

International Dialects of English Archive—www.dialectsarchive.com
Speech Accent Archive—http://accent.gmu.edu/
Irish Oral History Archive—http://www.ioha.co.uk/
Gaelic Athletic Association Oral History Project—www.bc.edu/centers/irish/gaahistory/Previous_Themes
Archives of Irish America/Ireland House Oral History Collection-NYU—http://www.nyu.edu/library/bobst/research/aia/collections/ihoral/oral01.php

YOUTUBE:

You can find a great deal of "region-specific" samples here, but you must be careful about the content of the clips you select. Also, be sure to verify that the speakers are actually from the region you are studying (some travel clips use professional narrators from other regions to narrate the regional clip).

FILMS:
Once
The Wind that Shakes the Barley
Rory O'Shea Was Here
Waking Ned Devine
Veronica Guerin
The Tiger's Tail
Intermission
The Boys & Girl From County Clare
Evelyn
The Closer You Get
About Adam
The Run of the Country
The Commitments
My Left Foot

TV:
    PBS Special—*The Irish in America*

C<small>DS</small>/C<small>OACHES</small>:
    Irish (vol. 1 & 2) Gillian Lane-Plescia
    Stage Dialects & More Stage Dialect Jerry Blunt

    For a more complete and detailed list of films/resources and a way to apply your knowledge to a role, see Ginny Kopf's book: *The Dialect Handbook*

Irish Monologues

Female

IRISH
MONOLOGUE
1 F

THE PLAY:
As a family buries their father, they realize that now they will live the rest of their lives under the hand of their mother—who has a debt to settle with all of them. Though their father abused her, they feared and revered him enough to keep to themselves—Katie even chose to take her father's side over her mother. Now, Maggie will do anything to get herself her long-deserved happiness—even at the cost of driving away her own children.

THE MONOLOGUE:
Katie (twenty-two) was her father's favorite. As the brothers and sisters grieve and plot to overcome the grip their mother has on their lives, futures, and fortunes, Katie provides more insight into the depth of their mother's cunning.

Time & Place:
Cork, Ireland. Evening. In the shop that Maggie now owns. After the counting of the day's receipts.

KATIE: You remember the time she caught him with Moll?

You remember our beloved mother was supposed to go to see that doctor in Dublin? [*her siblings nod 'yes'*]

She left here in a hired car at eight o'clock one night. She was to stay over night. You two and Mick had gone into town to a dance. I went to bed early that night because I was dying from the night before.

She didn't go to Dublin at all. She got the driver to turn round after dark and came straight back here. If I had known I could have tipped my father off.

I knew [Moll] had called to see him just after I went to bed but I knew nothing else. It could have been for anything. It could have been for the loan of money. You all know he couldn't say no. Besides her husband was in England and he wasn't sending her anything.

Moll arrived about ten o'clock. They spoke in whispers but I knew who it was. About twenty minutes after Moll's arrival I heard someone tiptoeing past my door and going on up the stairs to my father's room.

I opened my door and peeped out and I saw the back of her just outside my father's door. I nearly dropped dead. There was nothing I could do. She burst in the door and caught them red-handed.

Look! I saw Moll Sanders running down the stairs in her pelt and my mother after her. Is that enough for you?

IRISH
MONOLOGUE
1 F

THE PLAY:

As a family buries their father, they realize that now they will live the rest of their lives under the hand of their mother—who has a debt to settle with all of them. Though their father abused her, they feared and revered him enough to keep to themselves—Katie even chose to take her father's side over her mother. Now, Maggie will do anything to get herself her long-deserved happiness—even at the cost of driving away her own children.

THE MONOLOGUE:

Katie (twenty-two) was her father's favorite. She understood his need to cheat on their mother, and she tries to convince her siblings of their father's ultimate innocence.

TIME & PLACE:

Cork, Ireland. Evening. In the shop that Maggie now owns. After the counting of the day's receipts.

KATIE: Oh shut up. I didn't blame him.

For the love of God. My mother didn't sleep with him for years and when she did I doubt she was any good to him.

Oh grow up! I was at Cloonlara Races with him once and he was in the bar swopping yarns with a crowd of his cronies. I remember him to say that he was married for eighteen years and he never once saw his wife naked!

The bother with you is that you never tried to understand my father. All those men in the bar that night had the same story. They didn't know I was listening. The wives were too damn good. Damn them, they thought it was a sacrilege to fornicate with their own husbands.

DUBLIN CAROL

Conor McPherson

IRISH
MONOLOGUE
1 F

THE PLAY:
  Set in a mortician's office, the play centers around the life
of John . . . the mortician. In the first scene, he and his newest
recruit have just returned from a funeral and they chat lightly
around the heavy subject of life and death. In the second scene,
a bit of John's past returns to haunt him in the form of his grown
daughter who has come to bring John back to her dying mother
for a final goodbye. In the final scene, the young recruit returns
for his pay from the day before, and both men have taken too
much to drink as the world forces them to confront the issues
they truly wish they could bury.

THE MONOLOGUE:
  Mary (thirties) has returned to her estranged father after
ten years to try and convince him to visit her dying mother (his
dying wife). As the small talk finds its way into the heart of
the matter, Mary reveals a bit of her feelings about the way her
father's absence has affected her life.

TIME & PLACE:
  December 24. Present year. Early afternoon. The morti-
cian's office. "The north side of Dublin around Fairview or the
North Strand Road."

MARY: I had this boyfriend. He wasn't my boyfriend. I don't know what I was thinking. He was, this friend of mine at work, he was her brother. He was a big . . . they're from Kildare. He was a big culchie, teacher. Primary school teacher. I met him when we were out one night. There's this place, Major Tom's. I was. I just wanted something to happen. He was there. A big shiny red face. I didn't . . . I wasn't serious about him. I saw him a few times. Drinking stupid cocktails around those places up there around the center. And I just came up the steps with him one night, into the street. And whatever it was, the way the buildings looked, it took me back in time. And I felt that, you . . . I felt that you were with me. And this guy Ger, he was always pissed. He wanted me to go back to his house with him. And I know this is weird, but it was like he was, compared to you, even as a messer, compared to you, he was such a fucking amateur.

(They give a little laugh.)

Do you know? That even in the morning all he'd complain about would be his hangover and how he had copy books to correct. Where you'd be looking for money to hit the bottle . . .

(They are smiling a little, John shaking his head.)

Sometimes I smell you. Everything comes back.

IRISH
MONOLOGUE
1 F

THE PLAY:

An abstract theatrical telling of a familiar theme:

Boy goes off to seek his fortune in the world, boy returns home to find everything changed, boy falls in love, boy falls out of love and out of favor with the local authorities, boy is killed. Arthur Cleary left Dublin to do migrant work throughout Europe. His time away has aged him and he returns to his "home" to find it completely different. His age and mystique is attractive to Kathy (almost 15 years his junior) and she falls in love with him. When the local bully and the dirty cop realize he has returned and that he won't play along with the new order of things, he is beaten to death. All roles in the play except Arthur are played by 4 other people (2 men and 2 women) in interchanging roles.

THE MONOLOGUE:

Kathy/Girl (18) told her Friend that she would break things off with Arthur, but something prevented her from following through with the plan.

TIME & PLACE:

Present day. Dublin, Ireland. Exact location to be determined by the actors.

[Friend: Did you say goodbye to him like we agreed?]

KATHY: I did. (*She sits on the box as well.*) He was waiting for me along the quays, staring at the water like he always did. Didn't think I'd have the courage. "Arthur, I'm sorry," I said . . . "it's just too big a gap, it's not right." He never spoke, Sharon, his face looked old, suddenly, like all the air had drained from it. All the way home, felt like throwing myself from the bus. I came in, Sharon, saw my father, just sitting staring at the box. And I remembered a man who feared no other, a brown wage packet left on an oilskinned table. If he could only cry, I could stay with him, but his kind were never taught how to show grief. I need to learn to breathe. Sharon, I need Arthur and I don't know how to ask, to teach me . . . to wake up and not be afraid of what the day will bring. (*Pause.*) I've packed a bag, Sharon. If he'll take me in I'll go to him, or I'll go somewhere else, anywhere, but I don't fit here anymore. (*Pause.*) Will you be glad for me? I can't breathe here, Sharon. I'll see you the same, just . . . Sharon, please.

LEAVES

Lucy Caldwell

IRISH
MONOLOGUE
1 F

THE PLAY:

When their oldest daughter leaves for college, her family had no idea that she would become so depressed so quickly. After just three months of school, and without revealing it to anyone, she attempted suicide. This news rocked her sisters' and her parents' world and now they are left struggling to come to terms with the "why" of it all. When she returns home, after a visit to a hospital for recovery, her demeanor and inability to instantly change back into "normal" leaves her family in a state of confusion and anxiety.

THE MONOLOGUE:

Poppy (almost twelve) has been the only one in the family who seems actually excited that her sister Lori will be returning home—everyone else seems to be walking on egg shells. In her own way, and with the insight and perception of a young girl who can cut right to the heart of the adult mind, she talks to her mother about the books she has to read for school. In doing so, she offers up her own idea about how to "fix" the world in which they live.

TIME & PLACE:

Belfast, Northern Ireland. (*Note: this is a slightly different accent than the one taught in the introduction chapter, but a slight adjustment to the sound changes will solve that issue.*) Present day. Early evening. The living room of Poppy's house.

POPPY: Mum, do you think it's true that that would happen? All of—Well I haven't got to the end yet so I don't know exactly how things are going to turn out. But I mean—nuclear war and that—Tribulation they call it—I know it's never going to happen to us. But *if*—like if there was a nuclear war or a terrorist bomb or something—do you think that'd be what it was like?

I don't know—I mean—like—everyone fighting each other?

No, but you know what I mean. And do you think—do you think that people would actually start to become psychic? 'Cause I think—I mean I know the other people, the ones that can't do the thought-pictures and that, I know they're scared of it—but I think—Just imagine—Imagine knowing *exactly* how someone else was feeling.
     (silence)
What? *(beat)* I don't (know what you mean) . . . I just thought—You could tell someone exactly what you were feeling, or—like—show them how you were feeling. Wouldn't that be good? You'd be able to see exactly how happy or sad everyone else was. And so if they were feeling sad, you'd know, and you'd be able to—I mean—you know what to do, to make them better.

IRISH
MONOLOGUE
1 F

THE PLAY:

When their oldest daughter leaves for college, her family had no idea that she would become so depressed so quickly. After just three months of school, and without revealing it to anyone, she attempted suicide. This news rocked her sisters' and her parents' world and now they are left struggling to come to terms with the "why" of it all. When she returns home, after a visit to a hospital for recovery, her demeanor and inability to instantly change back into "normal" leaves her family in a state of confusion and anxiety.

THE MONOLOGUE:

Poppy (almost twelve) had been so excited to have her sister back at home. It's been two days and her sister has not seemed as excited to be home as Poppy believed she would be. She struggles to regain a sense of joy and peace again as she talks to her dad.

TIME & PLACE:

Belfast, Northern Ireland. (*Note: this is a slightly different accent than the one taught in the introduction chapter, but a slight adjustment to the sound changes will solve that issue*) Present day. Early evening. The living room of Poppy's house.

POPPY: I thought Lori being back would make things OK again. I really thought it would. (*silence*) Mum spoke to Lori the night before—the night before she—And she said that afterwards she went over and over the conversation in her head, trying to look for clues. But she said Lori just seemed—normal. There's no way of knowing what's actually going on in someone's head. We could all be sitting down at dinner and—it could just seem normal, but it wouldn't be, and none of us would know until afterwards, and even afterwards we wouldn't understand. And you can go over and over and over things in your head and still not know how to understand them. (*beat*)

How can anything ever be OK, Dad?

IRISH
MONOLOGUE
1 F

THE PLAY:

When their oldest daughter leaves for college, her family had no idea that she would become so depressed so quickly. After just three months of school, and without revealing it to anyone, she attempted suicide. This news rocked her sisters' and her parents' world and now they are left struggling to come to terms with the "why" of it all. When she returns home, after a visit to a hospital for recovery, her demeanor and inability to instantly change back into "normal" leaves her family in a state of confusion and anxiety.

THE MONOLOGUE:

Lori (nineteen) has been home for only a day and a half but it's been long enough to pack up her entire room and leave it completely bare . . . erasing all memories and mementoes from her childhood. As her mother checks in with her, she tries to get her mom to understand what has been going on inside her mind. Her mom does not seem able to help her in any way.

TIME & PLACE:

Belfast, Northern Ireland. (*Note: this is a slightly different accent than the one taught in the introduction chapter, but a slight adjustment to the sound changes will solve that issue.*) Present day. Early evening. Lori's room.

LORI: Mum? (*Phyllis [her mum] turns back quickly and sits down on the edge of the bed. She smoothes Lori's hair. Lori does not react.*)

Did you hear the helicopter last night?

I always think, you know—When you see pictures of—Of—Of—I don't know—of Iraq, or Kabul, or wherever—Places where there is real fighting going on—Helicopters overhead—that sort of thing—And remember the times when we were little and we couldn't sleep because of the helicopters? And I think of—I wonder if there are—and I mean there must be—other little children who can't sleep, and I wonder if their mothers are telling them to—ignore the sound, or to pretend it isn't there, like you used to do, so that they can get to sleep. And when I think about it, the thing is that I can't sleep, either. You know?

But Mum—How can you not think about it? And I don't mean—*you*—I mean—anyone—Once you've thought about it—once you've realized—How can anyone—*not* think about it?

Mum? Mum, do you think things get better?

I don't mean that, I don't mean me. I mean—things. Do you think that things—life—people—ever get better? (*beat*) Because I don't think they do. I'd like to think that—I'd like to be able to believe that things get better and people get happier but I don't think that's true.

I think—I think that things go on the way they always have been. I think that we think things change—or maybe we just have to believe they do—or pretend—I think that—yeah, sometimes people are happy—or think that they're happy—but I don't think they get happier. I don't think that things ever really get any better.

LEAVES

Lucy Caldwell

IRISH
MONOLOGUE
1 F

THE PLAY:
   When their oldest daughter leaves for college, her family had no idea that she would become so depressed so quickly. After just three months of school, and without revealing it to anyone, she attempted suicide. This news rocked her sisters' and her parents' world and now they are left struggling to come to terms with the "why" of it all. When she returns home, after a visit to a hospital for recovery, her demeanor and inability to instantly change back into "normal" leaves her family in a state of confusion and anxiety.

THE MONOLOGUE:
   Lori (nineteen) has been home for only a day and a half but it's been long enough to pack up her entire room and leave it completely bare . . . erasing all memories and mementoes from her childhood. Though her mother tries to give her a "pep talk" and encourage her, Lori's despair is deeply rooted in a sense of the futility of it all.

TIME & PLACE:
   Belfast, Northern Ireland. (*Note: this is a slightly different accent than the one taught in the introduction chapter, but a slight adjustment to the sound changes will solve that issue.*) Present day. Early evening. Lori's room.

LORI: *(carefully)* Mum—when I think of—of my grandparents, and their grandparents, and their grandparents, and back and back and back—and what, really, did they live and die and struggle and fight for? For the hope that things would get better? For the *(quote unquote)* "generations yet unborn"? For *me*? Because—because—in that case—if that's the case—then their lives, their deaths, everything—it was pointless. It was pointless, all of it, just—pointless. *(beat)* You see, Mum, there's nothing you can say.

No, but Mum—*(beat)* Once you've realized that—you can't go back to the way things were, because—Mum please—Don't cry, Mum, please—Mum—You need to listen, Mum because I need you to know this—I want to go back, I'd give anything—I want to believe in things the way I used to believe in them, the way I used to believe in them without even thinking about it—without even knowing that I *was* believing. But I can't, Mum, I can't—and it isn't even that it's I don't know *how* to, it's that I know I can't—and so I can't see how I can go on—go on—living —because—because—I don't think there's any such thing as the future, Mum. I think that life is just made up of moments, and outside each moment there's nothing else, and we have to believe that we're living in something bigger, something more coherent, because otherwise—otherwise we'd give up. I think that people need to believe that things get better—that one day, life on earth will be—beautiful— or else what would be the point of anything? It's like—it's like if you don't believe in heaven then you have to believe in earth—or you have to believe that heaven is a place you can find—or create—or whatever—on earth, but—and the only way I can say this, and you're not going to understand me, anyway, but the only way I can put it is that I don't believe in earth, either.

I'm sorry, Mum.

IRISH
MONOLOGUE
1 F

THE PLAY:

With the device of a narrator/commentator who doubles as the title character's daughter, the haunting story of a woman's devotion to the love of her life is told in flashback scenes and current-time monologues. Mai has never stopped loving her free-spirited musician husband who deserted her and their children while he toured around America and Europe looking for fame and success. While he is away, she builds a luxurious mansion on the most coveted site in the county—the shores of a mystical and beautiful lake— in the hopes that he will return to her. When he does return, much like the legend of the lake her home overlooks, Mai's "happy reunion" turns tragic.

THE MONOLOGUE:

On the day her father returns, Millie (sixteen) recounts the day he left them.

TIME & PLACE:

Summer 1979. Midlands Ireland. "A room with a huge bay window" overlooking Owl Lake. Late afternoon, early evening.

MILLIE: When I was eleven The Mai sent me into the butcher's to buy a needle and thread. It was the day Robert left us. No explanations, no goodbyes, he just got into his car with his cello and drove away. So The Mai and I went into town and sat in the Bluebell Hotel where The Mai downed six Paddys and red and I had six lemon-and-limes. Then The Mai turned to me with her sunglasses on, though it was the middle of winter, she turned to me and said, "Millie, would you ever run up to the butcher's and get me a needle and thread." Now at eleven I knew enough to know that needles and thread were bought in the drapery, but I thought maybe it was a special kind of thread The Mai wanted and because of the day that was in it I decided not to argue with her. So up I went to the butcher's and asked for a needle and a spool of thread and of course they didn't have any. Back I went to the Bluebell, sat beside The Mai and said rather gruffly, "Mom, they don't sell needles and thread in the butcher's." "Do they not, sweetheart?" The Mai whispered and started to cry. "Are you all right Mom?" I said. "I'm grand," she said. "Go up there and order me a Paddy and red." When I came back with the drinks The Mai said, "Don't you worry about a thing, Millie, your Dad'll come back and we will have the best of lives."

The Mai set about looking for that magic thread that would stitch us together again and she found it at Owl Lake, the most coveted site in the country. It was Sam Brady who sold the site to The Mai. For years he'd refused all offers, offers from hoteliers, publicans, restauranteurs, rich industrialists, Yanks, and then he turned round and gave it to The Mai for a song. When asked by irate locals why he'd sold it to The Mai, a blow-in, Sam merely answered, *"Highest bidder!"*

And so the new house was built and, once she had it the way she wanted, The Mai sat in front of this big window here, her chin moonward, a frown on her forehead, as if she were pulsing messages to some remote star which would ricochet and lance Robert wherever he was, her eyes closed tightly, her lips forming two words noiselessly. Come home—come home.

Kimberly Mohne Hill

IRISH
MONOLOGUE
1 F

THE PLAY:

With the device of a narrator/commentator who doubles as the title character's daughter, the haunting story of a woman's devotion to the love of her life is told in flashback scenes and current-time monologues. Mai has never stopped loving her free-spirited musician husband who deserted her and their children while he toured around America and Europe looking for fame and success. While he is away, she builds a luxurious mansion on the most coveted site in the county—the shores of a mystical and beautiful lake—in the hopes that he will return to her. When he does return, much like the legend of the lake her home overlooks, Mai's "happy reunion" turns tragic.

THE MONOLOGUE:

Millie (sixteen) remembers the effect her father's return had in the long-run—not just the momentary promises he made the summer he returned.

TIME & PLACE:

Summer 1979. Midlands Ireland. The study of a house looking out on Owl Lake. Evening.

MILLIE: (*watching them depart*) Maybe we did go into town the following day, I don't remember. It is beyond me now to imagine how we would've spent that day, where we would've gone, what we would've talked about, because when we meet now, which isn't often and always by chance, we shout and roar till we're exhausted or in tears or both, and then crawl away to lick our wounds already gathering venom for the next bout. We usually start with the high language. He'll fling the Fourth Commandment at me, HONOUR THY FATHER! And I'll hiss back, a father has to be honorable before he can be honored, or some facetious rubbish like that. And we'll pace ourselves like professionals, all the way to the last round, to the language of the gutter, where he'll call me a fuckin' cunt and I'll call him an ignorant bollix! We're well matched, neither ever gives an inch, we can't, it's life and death as we see it. And that's why I cannot remember that excursion into town if it ever occurred. What I do remember, however, is one morning a year and a half later when Robert and I drove into town to buy a blue nightgown and a blue bed-jacket for The Mai's waking. Still reeling from the terrible events of that weekend, we walked through the Midland drapery, the floorboards creaking, the other shoppers falling silent and turning away, they knew why we were there and what we'd come for, afraid to look yet needing to see, not wanting to move too closely lest they breathed in the damaged air of Owl Lake that hung about us like a wayward halo. No shroud for The Mai. It was her wish. In one of those throwaway conversations which only become significant with time, The Mai had said she wanted to be buried in blue. So here we were in a daze fingering sky blues, indigo blues, navy blues, lilac blues, night blues, finally settling on a watery blue silk affair. Business done, we moved down the aisle towards the door. A little boy, escaping his mother, ran from the side, banged off Robert and sent him backwards into a display stand.

About him on the floor, packets of needles and spools of thread all the colors of the rainbow.

IRISH
MONOLOGUE
1 F

THE PLAY:

With the device of a narrator/commentator who doubles as the title character's daughter, the haunting story of a woman's devotion to the love of her life is told in flashback scenes and current-time monologues. Mai has never stopped loving her free-spirited musician husband who deserted her and their children while he toured around America and Europe looking for fame and success. While he is away, she builds a luxurious mansion on the most coveted site in the county—the shores of a mystical and beautiful lake—in the hopes that he will return to her. When he does return, much like the legend of the lake her home overlooks, Mai's "happy reunion" turns tragic.

THE MONOLOGUE:

Millie (thirties) reflects on the lengths to which she went in order to escape the curse of Owl Lake.

TIME & PLACE:

Present/Past. Midlands Ireland. An evening. Millie's mother, Mai, is getting ready to attend a ball with her cheating husband.

MILLIE: Joseph, my five-year-old son, has never been to Owl Lake. I thought of having him adopted but would not part with him when the time came, and I'm glad, though I know it's hard for him. Already he is watchful and expects far too little of me, something I must have taught him unknown to myself. He is beginning to get curious about his father and I don't know what to tell him. I tell him all the good things. I say your daddy is an El Salvadorian drummer who swept me off my feet when I was lost in New York. I tell him his eyes are brown and his hair is black and that he loved to drink Jack Daniels by the neck. I tell him that high on hash or marijuana or god-knows-what we danced on the roof of a tenement building in Brooklyn to one of Robert's cello recordings.

I do not tell him that he is married with two sons to a jaded uptown society girl or that I tricked him into conceiving you because I thought it possible to have something for myself that didn't stink of Owl Lake. I do not tell him that on the day you were born, this jaded society queen sauntered into the hospital, chucked you under the chin, told me I was your daddy's last walk on the wild side, gave me a check for five thousand dollars and said, "You're on your own now, kiddo." And she was right. I had no business streelin' into her life, however tired it was. I do not tell him that, when you were two, I wrote a sensible letter, enclosing a photograph of you, asking him to acknowledge paternity. And I do not tell him he didn't answer.

MOLLY SWEENEY

Brian Friel

IRISH
MONOLOGUE
1 F

THE PLAY:
Mostly blind (she can detect only light and dark) since infancy, Molly Sweeney is given the hope of gaining her vision. Her husband persuades a visionary doctor to work with him to create a modern-medical miracle, and somewhere along the way, Molly is swept up in the hype. When the actual treatment occurs, and sight does visit her, Molly is not as balanced and excited as she had hoped, or the others had envisioned.

THE MONOLOGUE:
As throughout the play, the characters take turns revealing the inner-workings of their minds and motivations. After her operation, Molly (thirties) had a bit of a breakdown and found herself back in a familiar place . . . the same psychiatric hospital in which her mother had been a patient for a short time. Molly recalls the hospital.

TIME & PLACE:
The (fictional) town of Ballybeg, County Donegal.

MOLLY: During all those years when my mother was in the hospital with her nerves my father brought me to visit her only three times. Maybe that was her choice. Or his. I never knew.

But I have a vivid memory of each of those three visits.

One of the voice of a youngish woman. My father and mother are in her ward, surrounded by a screen fighting as usual, and I'm standing outside in the huge echoey corridor. And I can hear a young woman sobbing at the far end of the corridor. More lamenting than sobbing. And even though a lot of people are passing along that corridor I remember wondering why nobody paid any attention to her. And for some reason the sound of that lamentation stayed with me.

And I remember another patient, an old man, leaning over me and enveloping me in the smell of snuff. He slipped a coin into my hand and said, "Go out and buy us a fancy new car, son, and the two of us will drive away to beautiful Fethard-on-Sea." And he laughed. He had given me a shilling.

And the third memory is of my mother sitting on the side of her bed, shouting at my father, screaming at him, "She should be at a blind school! You know she should! But you know the real reason you won't send her? Not because you haven't the money. Because you want to punish me."

I didn't tell Mr. Rice that story when he first asked me about my childhood. Out of loyalty to father, maybe. Maybe out of loyalty to mother, too.

Anyhow those memories came into my head the other day. I can't have been more than six or seven at the time.

IRISH
MONOLOGUE
1 F

THE PLAY:

Oweney owns a small, old-fashioned barber shop in a run-down section of an Irish town. Above his shop are rooms that he rents out to a local artist and a young man who was recently let go from the hotel that closed up across the street. Oweney's regular patrons include the "heavy" for the local loan shark and a friend whose wife is in an insane asylum nearby. When the loan shark's wife, Maeve, opens her boutique shop across the street, Oweney's long distance crush on her begins to move in a more dangerously close direction.

THE MONOLOGUE:

Maeve (thirties) has grown closer to Oweney, deceiving her husband (P.J.). Her desire to make her own way in the world and gain back a bit of the power that her husband seems content to take from her drive her to reveal her vulnerabilities to Oweney.

TIME & PLACE:

Oweney's barber shop. A small town in Ireland. Night.

MAEVE: I used to think PJ's silence meant he was mysterious but I'm not so sure anymore now . . . I hate that house Oweney. It's like livin' in a fortress I swear—alarms and cameras and all the rest of it. He says there's a limit to the time I can keep the shop too, that if I don't make a go of it fairly soon he's goin' to take it back from me. He thinks that'll stop me but it won't. 'Cause I want to do somethin' Oweney, yeh know. I want to be someone—in my own right! Yeh know? Not just attached to someone else all the time. I know that probably makes me sound like a bit of a bitch and all but I don't care . . . Mind you, I'll probably only be gettin' on my feet when he'll want to move again. 'Cause he never stays put. When he's here he wants to be there. When he's there he wants to be somewhere else. And he wants to knock everything down—the house where he was born in case somebody sees it, the old hotel for spite, the whole neighborhood if necessary. Anything but stand still. Sure we had a lovely little orchard at the back of the house and he tore it down to build a pool room. And he don't even play pool like! . . . I mean I don't really know anyone any more Oweney, yeh know. I mean I've no real friends or anything. And I'm not sayin' it's all PJ's fault or anythin'. It's not. It's mine. I mean I'm probably not whatdoyoucallit . . . I don't know . . . likeable or somethin'!

    (going to him)

Do yeh know what I mean though Oweney?

IRISH
MONOLOGUE
1 F

THE PLAY:

In this dark and mournful play, Portia is haunted by the death of her twin brother 15 years ago, and on her 30th birthday it all comes back full force. Her friends, family, and husband see that she is not herself—something about turning 30 has pushed Portia over the edge. The relationships she has with her friends, lovers, husband, children and parents are cut to the core as the truth about the past is revealed and the circumstances of the present come to a climax.

THE MONOLOGUE:

Portia (thirty) confronts her mother about the death of her twin brother and its effect on the rest of Portia's life.

TIME & PLACE:

Late afternoon. Portia's living room. Ireland.
Present-day. Portia's birthday.

PORTIA: You'd like that, wouldn't ya, weepin' at the grave of one of your darlin' grandsons. Be history repeatin' itself, wouldn't it now, be like buryin' Gabriel all over again. I know how your bitter mind works, you think that if one of my sons was drowned that maybe ya could explain away how me twin was lost. Well, Mother, nothin'll ever explain that, nothin'.

I read subtext, Mother, words dropped be accident, phrases covered over, sentences unfinished, and I know the topography of your mind as well as I know every inch and ditch and drain of Belmont Farm, so don't you bluster in here and put a death wish on my sons just because you couldn't save your own. My sons'll be fine for if I do nothin' else I leave them alone and no mark is better than a black one.

He would've been thirty today as well—sometimes I think only half of me is left, the worst half. Do ya know the only reason I married Raphael? Not because you and Daddy says I should, not because he was rich, I care nothin' for money, naw. The only reason I married Raphael was because of his name, an angel's name, same as Gabriel's, and I thought be osmosis or just pure wishin' that one'd take on the qualities of the other. But Raphael is not Gabriel and never will be—And I dreamt about him again last night, was one of them dreams as is so real you think it's actually happenin'. Gabriel had come to dinner here and after he got up to leave and I says, "Gabriel, stay for the weekend," but Gabriel demurs out of politeness to me and Raphael. And I says, "Gabriel, it's me, Portia, your twin, don't be polite, there's no need with me"—And then he turns and smiles and I know he's goin' to stay and me heart blows open and stars falls out of me chest as happens in dreams - We were so alike, weren't we, Mother?

Came out of the womb holdin' hands—When God was handin' out souls he must've got mine and Gabriel's mixed up, aither that or he gave us just the one between us and it went into the Belmont River with him—Oh, Gabriel, ya had no right to discard me so, to float me on the world as if I were a ball of flotsam. Ya had no right, *(begins to weep uncontrollably)*

IRISH
MONOLOGUE
1 F

THE PLAY:
In this dark and mournful play, Portia is haunted by the death
of her twin brother 15 years ago, and on her 30th birthday it all
comes back full force. Her friends, family, and husband see that
she is not herself—something about turning 30 has pushed Portia
over the edge. The relationships she has with her friends, lovers,
husband, children and parents are cut to the core as the truth about
the past is revealed and the circumstances of the present come to
a climax.

THE MONOLOGUE:
    Portia (thirty) confesses the truth about her brother's death
to the local "professional woman"—her friend Maggie May.

TIME & PLACE:
    Late afternoon. The bank of the Belmont River. Ireland.
Present-day. Portia's birthday.

PORTIA: Suppose he's not there when I go?

Before I was always sure, was the one thing as kept me goin'—Now I don't know anymore, and yet I know that somewhere he lives and that's the place I want to be.

There's a wolf tooth growin' in me heart and it's turnin' me from everyone and everythin' I am. I wishin' if the wind or somethin' would carry me from this place without me havin' to do anythin' meself.

I knew he was goin' to do it, planned to do it together, and at the last minute I got afraid and he just went on in and I called him back but he didn't hear me on account of the swell and just kept on wadin', and I'm standin' on the bank, right here, shoutin' at him to come back and at the last second he turns thinkin' I'm behind him, his face, Maggie May, the look on his face, and he tries to make the bank but the undertow do have him and a wave washes over him—

They don't like to talk about Gabriel. No one does. Don't know if anyone knows what it's like to be a twin. Everythin's swapped and mixed up and you're aither two people or you're no one. He used to call me Gabriel and I used to call him Portia. Times we got so confused we couldn't tell who was who and we'd have to wait for someone else to identify us and put us back into ourselves. I could make him cry be just callin' him Portia. We didn't really like one another that much when it came down to it. Oh, how can everyone be alive and not him? If I could just see him, just once, I'd be alright, I know I would.

THE SANCTUARY LAMP

Tom Murphy

IRISH
MONOLOGUE
1 F

THE PLAY:

Set in a Sanctuary, three main characters come together seeking sanctuary from their lives and their sordid pasts. Under the constant, loving, never-ceasing glow of the "sanctuary lamp," the three reveal their demons and their hope for forgiveness.

THE MONOLOGUE:

Maudie (fifteen-sixteen) has snuck out of her grandparents' house, again, and has run away to the church to get relief from the images that haunt her at home. Her dead mother and her dead baby come to her in her dreams, and she seeks forgiveness for the sins that she committed which took them away from her. Here, she reveals the way in which she "sees" her mom.

TIME & PLACE:

After 10 p.m., in the sanctuary of "a church in a city." Ireland. Present day.

MAUDIE: *My* mam? *My* mam is dead. When did she die? (*she smiles.*) I think it were a few years ago.

Well, do you know "dreaming"? Do you? Well, I don't know. I never saw my mam. Not that I remember. I saw my dad alright, but I never saw my mam. They went their separate ways, gran said. Well, a few years ago, I started to—dream—about my mam. Then I knew she were dead. But I think she were really visiting me. But gran said, dreaming. But I don't agree. But gran said "dreaming, Maudie, dreaming" and not to be dementing her and not let grandad hear. (*She looks at Harry for his appraisal. Note: to Maudie, this story is essentially one of personal triumph.*)

Well, do you know "in bed"? Yes. Her face would come beside me, in the dark, like a plate. And her eyes would look at me. And I didn't know what to say. So then I'd look about for gran. Or even grandad. To say something. But when I'd look around again, my mam were always gone. And then I'd try to scream. To fill the room again. But I couldn't scream. And it went on like that. Like, every night. Like, forever. Well, one night, I knew there were a change. She were not staring at me anymore. She were looking down. More peaceful. Like reading the paper. Or thinking it out. And I looked about to see if gran had seen this change for the better. Gran had seen alright, but she wouldn't pretend. And I knew that when I'd look around again my mam would still be there. And she were. And I waited. But then my mam got up—(*Maudie gives a haughty toss of her hair.*) My mam got up and went out. I were so disappointed. I think I were going to cry. But then the door opened again and my mam were standing there, and she looked at no one else, and she said, "Oh, by the way, Maudie, I'm very happy now." And I were so grateful. And then I told my gran, whether it were dreaming or not, it were all over.

IRISH
MONOLOGUE
1 F

THE PLAY:

Set in a Sanctuary, three main characters come together seeking sanctuary from their lives and their sordid pasts. Under the constant, loving, never-ceasing glow of the "sanctuary lamp," the three reveal their demons and their hope for forgiveness.

THE MONOLOGUE:

Maudie (fifteen-sixteen) has snuck out of her grandparents' house, again, and has run away to the church to get relief from the images that haunt her at home. Her dead mother and her dead baby come to her in her dreams, and she seeks forgiveness for the sins that she committed which took them away from her. Here, she reveals the truth behind her secret past and the birth and the death of her son.

TIME & PLACE:

After 10 p.m., in the sanctuary of "a church in a city." Ireland. Present day.

[Francisco: Did he die? Did you have him adopted?]

MAUDIE: . . . Shall I tell you? Do you know—hospitals?
Well, my grandad said let someone else take care of me.
Well, I come home late one night and he were waiting. In
the hall. In his bare feet. And he found eight new p. in my
pocket. *I* don't know how it got there. Maybe one of the
bigger boys. And grandad said he would have kicked me,
if he had his boots on. And grandad said let someone else
take care of me to have a baby. And gran was lucky to find
me one of those hospitals. And I had a baby. I knew he were
not well. But I knew if I could not take care of him, who
could? And once I woke and they were taking him away.
And I growled. But there were an old—Do you know nuns?
Well, there were an old nun. She were in black, the others
were in white, and she were my friend. And she said had I
thought of a name for him. I hadn't thought of a name. And
she said would I call him Stephen. Because that were her
name. And she would like that. And I said okay. And they
smiled—the way I said "okay." And I laughed. But I were
not happy at all. But I were so warm and sleepy. I wanted
to sit up so they'd see I were not happy. Because I were
crying. So they took him away to baptize him. Because he
were not well. And the next time I woke up, only the old
nun were there. And she come to me, sort of smiling and
frowning together. And said "Maudie. Maudie." Like that.
Like as if I were asleep. But I were awake. I were wide
awake. And she said, "Stephen is dead, Maudie. Stephen
is with Jesus."At first I didn't know if she were only fib-
bing, but when he started to visit me—No, not dreaming!
Not dreaming! So all around me!—I knew he were dead
alright. but I didn't tell them. Because I wanted them to let
me go. And I didn't want the other patients to pull my hair.
I only told the old nun. To ask her would it stop. And she
said it would, in time. And I said, when I got forgiveness,
was it? And she said yes.

TRANSLATIONS

Brian Friel

Irish
Monologue
1 F

The Play:

Set in Baile Beag, Donegal in North West Ireland, the play confronts the issue of "conquerors" and the "conquered" and the ensuing eradication of language and culture of the original inhabitants of a land. One of the locals, Owen, has been hired (conscripted?) by the British military to translate the place names of the region for the creation of a new, anglicized map. Believing he is doing a good deed, and happy for the money he is being paid, he soon realizes that he has actually sold out his own people to the enemy. The locals do not give in without a fight, though, with tragic consequences for an innocent British soldier and his Irish love.

The Monologue:

Maire Chatach (*twenties*) has fallen in love with a British soldier who is working on the mapping project. Though they never understood each other's language, they managed to find common ground in their feelings for one another. After their night together, he goes missing. Entering the hedge school with the vain hope that he will be there, she seeks comfort from her friends as she relives the wonderful night with him.

Time & Place:

A hedge school in a barn in Donegal, Ireland.

MAIRE CHATACH: He left me home, Owen. And the last thing he said to me—he tried to speak in Irish—he said, "I'll see you yesterday"—he meant to say "I'll see you tomorrow." And I laughed that much he pretended to get cross and he said "Maypoll! Maypoll!" because I said that word wrong. And off he went, laughing—laughing, Owen! Do you think he's alright? What *do* you think?

He comes from a tiny place called Winfarthing.
(she suddenly drops on her hands and knees on the floor—where Owen had his map a few minutes ago— and with her finger traces an outline map)
Come here till you see. Look. There's Winfarthing. And there's two other wee villages right beside it; one of them's called Barton Bendish—it's there; and the other's called Saxingham Nethergate—it's about there. And there's Little Walsingham—that's his mother's townland. Aren't they odd names? Sure they make no sense to me at all. And Winfarthing's near big town called Norwich. And Norwich is in a county called Norfolk. And Norfolk is in the east of England. He drew a map for me on the wet strand and wrote the names on it. I have it all in my head now. Winfarthing—Barton Bendish—Saxingham Nethergate—Little Walsingham— Norwich—Norfolk. Strange sounds, aren't they? But nice sounds; like Jimmy Jack reciting his Homer.
(she gets to her feet and looks around; she is almost serene now. To Sarah:)
You were looking lovely last night, Sarah. Is that the dress you got from Boston? Green suits you.
(to Owen)
Something very bad's happened to him, Owen, I know. He wouldn't go away without telling me. Where is he, Owen? You're his friend—where is he?

Kimberly Mohne Hill   115

MALE

IRISH
MONOLOGUE
1 M

THE PLAY:

An abstract theatrical telling of a familiar theme:

Boy goes off to seek his fortune in the world, boy returns home to find everything changed, boy falls in love, boy falls out of love and out of favor with the local authorities, boy is killed. Arthur Cleary left Dublin to do migrant work throughout Europe. His time away has aged him and he returns to his "home" to find it completely different. His age and mystique is attractive to Kathy (almost 15 years his junior) and she falls in love with him. When the local bully and the dirty cop realize he has returned and that he won't play along with the new order of things, he is beaten to death. All roles in the play except Arthur are played by 4 other people (2 men and 2 women) in interchanging roles.

THE MONOLOGUE:

Arthur (thirties) is looking out the window of his flat at the local neighborhood "boss"—a bully named Deignan. His childhood memories of the man only stir his hatred further, leading towards his inevitable end. Here, he remembers how the man carefully cultivated his social status.

TIME & PLACE:

Present day. Dublin, Ireland. Arthur's flat. Early evening.

ARTHUR: He's out there again. Deignan. *(bitterly)* God, I remember him now, a little brat in short trousers, perpetual snot on his nose and even then he could buy and sell you. He used to steal sweets from the mother and flog them for half price. Then when we were fourteen . . . I remember . . . it was Johnnies. Don't know where he got them, but he told the whole school I'd bought four off him one evening and came back the next day for two. Jaysus, they were buying them by the newtide, every penny they had . . . hidden under beds, going green, never used . . . and back next week for more in case he'd tell people they hadn't needed them.

Before I went away I saw him one night . . . Monkstown . . . all the little rich kids with money and no sense. He was selling them joints, ready-rolled for half a crown. They were having to be carried home to Mammy by their friends. I took a pull . . . herbal tobacco and loose shag . . . he winked up at me: "Do you want a cut Arthur, be my man here." Christ, he looked pathetic, the elephant flares, huge tie like a red carpet. *(he pauses and his tone changes)* I saw him yesterday in Drumcondra. Collecting rent. He's four houses there in flats. Warrens. You should have seen the number of bells on every door. That Doyle woman is with him. Like a dog keeping its distance, terrified of a kick.

The Lament for Arthur Cleary

Dermot Bolger

Irish
Monologue
1 M

The Play:

An abstract theatrical telling of a familiar theme:

Boy goes off to seek his fortune in the world, boy returns home to find everything changed, boy falls in love, boy falls out of love and out of favor with the local authorities, boy is killed. Arthur Cleary left Dublin to do migrant work throughout Europe. His time away has aged him and he returns to his "home" to find it completely different. His age and mystique is attractive to Kathy (almost 15 years his junior) and she falls in love with him. When the local bully and the dirty cop realize he has returned and that he won't play along with the new order of things, he is beaten to death. All roles in the play except Arthur are played by 4 other people (2 men and 2 women) in interchanging roles.

The Monologue:

Arthur (thirties) comforts his girlfriend after she has another nightmare about Arthur's death. As he lists the places he's been, he begins to reflect on the way he came to be where he is today, and why his life didn't turn out the way he thought it would.

Time & Place:

Arthur's flat. Night time. Present day. Dublin, Ireland.

ARTHUR: *(teasing softly)* Capel Street, Rialto, Phibsborough . . .
(quietly, soothing) Altone. Blankensse, with little cobbled steps
and terrace cafes built on jetties onto the Albe that would rock
in the wake of the boats passing. Wedel where the ships would
play their national anthems as they left the mouth of the river.
And the dormitories. Always the same. That time my ribs
were cracked in the strike of foreign pickers and I lay for a
week in the third bunk up, staring at the streets of Dublin
tattooed along the veins of my wrist. The stink of Turkish
cigarettes, photos of kids, pin-ups, and always at night the
same talk of returning, even if you couldn't follow the languages, you knew what they were talking about.

[*Girl: And then you came back. You never told me why
Arthur.*]

(pause) Can't really explain it. Just happened one night,
halted at a border post. Lines of tracks, containers stacked on
sidings. I'd pulled the window down to watch a guard shining his light under the train when suddenly I was overcome
with longing for something . . . I don't know . . . something
I'd lost . . . (pause) I keep thinking I've found it and it slips
away again. Could have been that way forever, drifting from
city to city. Only something happened at that border post.
I saw my reflection in the window . . . so suddenly old, so
stale with experience. I felt this panic I couldn't explain . . .
that if I stayed in the carriage I would be damned to wander
forever across that continent. The guard had stamped my
passport and made the usual joke. I was alone. I turned the
door handle and jumped, began to run as the official with the
torch shouted after me. I never looked back, just dodged past
shunting wagons and containers till I reached the gates and
was out into the countryside. There was woodland, through
the foliage I could see lights of trucks from an autobahn.
I kept running until I came to what I thought was a ruined
house. When I got closer I realized it was a war monument,
the shell of a building where people had been shot. I smoked
cigarettes all night leaning again the plaque, clutching the
battered green passport in my hands. Next morning I hitched
to the nearest port, caught a ferry to Holland, a plane from
there. Island's Eye, Lambay, wheeling over Swords so huge
below me it was hard to believe I was home.

Kimberly Mohne Hill

IRISH
MONOLOGUE
1 M

THE PLAY:

Set during World War I, and referencing one of the bloodiest, deadliest battles of that war, "the Sons of Ulster" follows a group of Irishmen sent overseas to fight for their land and their religion. As they sense their youth slipping away from them, and they smell the scent of impending death, they relive the stories and songs and prayers of their homeland.

THE MONOLOGUE:

On a weekend break, the young warriors have split off into pairs to enjoy themselves and come to terms with the last bit of bloodshed they have just witnessed. Pyper (twenties) was saved by Craig, and the two men have retreated to Craig's favorite island, Boa Island. Pyper tells the truth about the woman "he married because he was curious" when he was last in France.

TIME & PLACE:

Boa Island, Lough Erne, Northern Ireland. World War I.

[Craig: Why'd you kill her?]

PYPER: I had to. And she killed herself.

She killed herself. She killed herself. She killed herself. Because she was stupid enough to believe that I was all she had to live for. Me. What would I have brought her? The same end, but a lot later, and not with the dignity of doing it with her own hand. I'm one of the gods, I bring destruction. Remember?

What's more to be said? She took her life. She did something with it, finally and forever. I thought I was doing the same when I cleared out of this country and went to do something with my heart and my eyes and my hands and my brains. Something I could not do here as the eldest son of a respectable family whose greatest boast is that in their house Sir Edward Carson, savior of their tribe, danced in the finest gathering Armagh had ever seen. I escaped Carson's dance. While you were running with your precious motors to bring in his guns, I escaped Carson's dance, David. I got out to create, not destroy. But the gods wouldn't allow that. I could not create. That's the real horror of what I found in Paris, not the corpse of a dead whore. I couldn't look at my life's work, for when I saw my hands working, they were not mine but the hands of my ancestors, interfering, and I could not be rid of that interference. I could not create. I could only preserve. Preserve my flesh and blood, what I'd seen, what I'd learned. It wasn't enough. I was contaminated. I smashed my sculpture and I rejected any woman who would continue my breed. I destroyed one to make that certain. And I would destroy my own life. I would take up arms at the call of my Protestant fathers. I would kill in their name and I would die in their name. To win their respect would be my sole act of revenge, revenge for the bad joke they had played on me in making me sufficiently different to believe I was unique, when my true uniqueness lay only in how alike them I really was.

Observe the Sons of Ulster Marching Towards the Somme
Frank McGuinness

IRISH
MONOLOGUE
1 M

THE PLAY:

Set during World War I, and referencing one of the bloodiest, deadliest battles of that war, "the Sons of Ulster" follows a group of Irishmen sent overseas to fight for their land and their religion. As they sense their youth slipping away from them, and they smell the scent of impending death, they relive the stories and songs and prayers of their homeland.

THE MONOLOGUE:

On a weekend break, the young warriors have split off into pairs to enjoy themselves and come to terms with the last bit of bloodshed they have just witnessed. Crawford (twenties) has come with the "preacher," Roulston, to his old church. As Roulston cowers in the church, praying and trying to get Crawford to let him quit the army, Crawford does what it takes to give Roulston back his fighting edge.

TIME & PLACE:

A church in Northern Ireland. World War I.

CRAWFORD: Who cares? *(silence)* Who cares what you think you are? I don't give a damn. What kind of boy do you think I am? You seem to think I'm soft in the head. Just like Anderson and McIlwaine did on the first day to me, you're doing now. Trying to knock the living daylights out of my mind and senses—through ganging up. They ganged up with each other. You gang up with Christ. Well, listen, keep him to yourself. I'm not interested in either of you. Christ never did much for me, and I don't think he's done much for you. What did he give me? Look at it. What am I? I'll tell you. I'm a soldier that risks his neck for no cause other than the men he's fighting with. I've seen enough to see through empires and kings and countries. I know the only side worth supporting is your own sweet self. I'll support you because if it comes to the crunch I hope you'll support me. That's all I know. That's all I feel. I don't believe in Christ. I believe in myself. I believe in you only in so far as you're a soldier like myself. No more, no less. That's what I have to say about your outburst. It was a disgrace. Do you have anything to say to defend yourself?

Irish
Monologue
1 M

THE PLAY:
Oweney owns a small, old-fashioned barber shop in a run-down section of an Irish town. Above his shop are rooms that he rents out to a local artist and a young man who was recently let go from the hotel that closed up across the street. Oweney's regular patrons include the "heavy" for the local loan shark and a friend whose wife is in an insane asylum nearby. When the loan shark's wife, Maeve, opens her boutique shop across the street, Oweney's long distance crush on her begins to move in a more dangerously close direction.

THE MONOLOGUE:
Leonard (late teens-early twenties) talks to Matt (twenties-the artist) while his portrait is being painted.

TIME & PLACE:
A room above a barber shop. Small town Ireland. Present day. Morning.

LEONARD: *(Leonard is sitting on a chair while Matt stands behind his easel, painting a portrait of him)* The nun brought us all down to the picture house to see *The Ten Commandments*. We were marched through the town in twos. I was holdin' me little sister's hand so tight I must have been nearly hurtin' her. But I was afraid of my life I was goin' to lose her, like yeh know. In me own hometown! Anyway some of the local lads started jeerin' us as we were standin' in the queue—callin' us names and that. I tried to explain to one of them that meself and Bernadette shouldn't really be in St. Mary's at all—that our Mammy and Daddy were still alive—but he wouldn't listen to me. They let us into the picture for half price, put us sittin' in the hard seats. They might as well have put a big placard around our necks. Even to this day I can't buy anything for half price. The gas thing about it all though is that no one saw the funny side to it. I mean bringin' a crowd of orphans to a picture that began with a woman rollin' her baby down the river in a basket.

(Leonard chuckles)

I was seven. Bernadette was five. I knew straight away that we were in trouble. I mean I knew we weren't goin' to be able to pull out of it that easy or anything. Me da started drinkin' and then six months later we were taken into care.

Yeah, he used to come up most Sundays, like. But he was usually half jarred and that. In the end he more or less stopped comin' altogether.

On Such as We

Billy Roche

IRISH
MONOLOGUE
1 M

THE PLAY:

Oweney owns a small, old-fashioned barber shop in a run-down section of an Irish town. Above his shop are rooms that he rents out to a local artist and a young man who was recently let go from the hotel that closed up across the street. Oweney's regular patrons include the "heavy" for the local loan shark and a friend whose wife is in an insane asylum nearby. When the loan shark's wife, Maeve, opens her boutique shop across the street, Oweney's long distance crush on her begins to move in a more dangerously close direction.

THE MONOLOGUE:

Eddie (twenties) has just been sent to retrieve a painting that Matt painted of the street outside Oweney's window. It has Maeve and her boutique in it (though you can only barely see her in the distance) and Matt had given it to Oweney as payment for rent. When Maeve's husband learned of Oweney's interest in his wife, he sent Eddie to "buy" the painting back . . . by force, if necessary. Here, Eddie justifies his actions to the rest of the barber shop regulars as he exits with the painting. *[Caution: this monologue has strong language]*

TIME & PLACE:

Oweney's barber shop. A small town in Ireland. Late afternoon.

EDDIE: Better I caught yeh unawares Oweney. If you knew it was comin' you'd've only tightened up on me and I'd've cracked a rib on yeh or somethin'. Are yeh alright? Try and straighten up now . . . That's it. Go over to the window Oweney . . . Now you're learnin' . . . Where's the paintin'?—down in the room? Yeah? . . . Answer it will yeh! (*the phone*)

> (*Eddie [gets] the painting*)

I'll leave your money here Oweney. Look. Alright? I don't know what you're makin' such a fuss about anyway; you can hardly even make her out in it.

> (*he goes to Matt*)

And listen here you, in future you pay that man his rent in hard cash. Never mind your paintin's. Yeh can't eat a paintin' yeh know and that man has a wife and family to support. So in future you pay him in cash and be done with it. And don't tell me yeh haven't got it either. You get the dole and your rent allowance the same as the rest of us. So hand it over. 'Cause if I find out that you haven't paid him his rent I'll come up there and wreck the place on yeh and I'll throw you out through the fuckin' window. Yeh fuckin' little prick yeh! Don't go makin' a big deal out of this now Oweney . . .

> (*he goes to Leonard in the hall*)

You wanted a loan of a hundred. PJ said yes. But first I want to know what you want it for? Yeah, right . . . . Here and don't spend it all in the one shop. And remember when I come lookin' for this you better have somethin' for me. Right? . . . It's better this way Oweney. Better for you, better for me, better for everyone. Anyway—faraway women and all the rest of it Oweney yeh know. Faraway women boy!

IRISH
MONOLOGUE
1 M

THE PLAY:

It's a dark and stormy Christmas eve in Howth, Dublin, Ireland. Cranky, blind Richard and his recovering-alcoholic brother Sharky prepare for a normal evening at home. They are joined by their recently-kicked-out-of-the-house drunken friend, Ivan. Shortly after, another friend, Nicky arrives with a stranger for a Christmas-eve game of poker. It's a party! The only problem is, the stranger is actually the Devil who is there to claim Sharky's soul. Will the Devil leave victorious or will someone redeem Sharky's soul? It's a true Christmas story in an unconventional setting!

THE MONOLOGUE:

The Devil (ageless), in the body of "Mr. Lockhart" has been toying with Sharky all night. As they consume more and more liquor, the Devil's human body begins to show the signs of intoxication—surprising to the non-human Devil. As the physical body reveals its limitations, the Devil reveals the more eternal limitations he must endure forever. Sharky's question, "what will happen to me . . . if I lose?" sparks this tragic, horrifying, touching response.

TIME & PLACE:

Close to midnight. Christmas Eve. Howth, Dublin, Ireland. The present. The basement living room/poker room of Richard and Sharky's home.

LOCKHART (the devil): What's hell? (*gives a little laugh*) Hell is . . . (*stares gloomily*) Well, you know, Sharky, when you're walking round and round the city and the streetlights have all come on and it's cold. Or your standing outside a shop where you were hanging around reading the magazines, pretending to buy one 'cause you've no money and nowhere to go and your feet are like blocks of ice in those stupid little slip-on shoes you bought for chauffeuring. And you see all the people who seem to live in another world all snuggled up together in the warmth of a tavern or a cozy little house, and you just walk and walk and walk and you're on your own and nobody knows who you are. And you don't know anyone and you're trying not to hassle people or beg, because you're trying not to drink, and you're hoping you *won't* meet anyone you know because of the blistering shame that rises up in your face and you have to turn away because you know you can't even deal with the thought that someone might love you, because of all the pain you always cause. Well that's a fraction of the self-loathing you feel in hell, except it's worse. Because there truly is no one to love you. Not even Him. *(points to the sky)* He lets you go. Even He's sick of you. You're locked in a space that's smaller than a coffin. Which is lying a thousand miles down just under the bed of a vast, icy, pitch black sea. You're buried alive in there. And it's so cold that you can't even feel your angry tears freezing in your eyelashes and your very bones ache with deep perpetual agony and you think, "I must be going to die . . ." But you never die. You never even sleep because every few minutes you're gripped by a claustrophobic panic and you get so frightened you squirm uselessly against the stone walls and the heavy lid, and your heart beats so fast against your ribs you think, "I *must* be going to die . . . " But of course . . . you never will. Because of what you did. *(pause)* That's where I am too, Sharky. I know you see me here in this man's clothes, but that's where I really am . . . *(short pause)* Oh you'd have loved heaven, Sharky. It's *unbelievable*! Everyone feels peaceful! *(laughs)* Everyone feels at such peace! Because your mind is at one with the infinite. *(Darker)* At a certain point each day music plays. It seems to emanate from the very sun itself. Not so much a tune as a heartbreakingly beautiful vibration in the sunlight shining down on and through all the souls. A blanket of clear, almost unthinkable, harmonies. It's so moving you wonder how you could ever have doubted anything as you think back on this painful life which is just a sad distant memory. Time just slips away in heaven, Sharky. But not for you. No. You are about to find out that time is bigger and blacker and so much more boundless than you could ever have thought possible with your puny broken mind.

Kimberly Mohne Hill   131

SIVE

John B. Keane

IRISH
MONOLOGUE
1M

THE PLAY:
Sive, the title character, is being raised by her dead mother's
brother (Uncle Mike) and his climbing, scheming wife. Sive's
grandma is her closest ally and she helps Sive develop a relationship with the local boy, Liam Scuab. Liam loves Sive, but
her uncle does not approve of him. No one is going to be good
enough for her, but Mike bows to his wife's wishes and allows
the local matchmaker to arrange a marriage between Sive and
the oldest, richest man in town. When all else fails, and everyone
betrays her, Sive tragically does the only thing she can think of
to prevent the despicable union from taking place.

THE MONOLOGUE:
Liam Scuab (nineteen) pleads with Sive's uncle and aunt
not to marry her off (sell her off, actually) to the oldest man in
the village. Liam is deeply in love with Sive and she loves him,
but the greed of her caretakers threatens her happiness.

TIME & PLACE:
Late 1950's. Rural Ireland. Sive's home.

LIAM: (*pleading*) In the honor of God, I beseech you to forget about violence. I tell you I want no trouble. If I have upset ye, I'm sorry, but surely if ye know God ye must think of this terrible auction. Ye must know that a day will dawn for all of us when an account must be given. Do not think of me. I promise I will leave these parts till Sive is a woman. I swear that on my dead mother. But do not give her to that rotting old man with his gloating eyes and trembling hands.

Think, woman, I beg of you! Think, Mike Glavin! Forget about yourselves and see it with good eyes instead of greedy ones. Have you knowledge of the Crucified Son of God? (*shakes his head with emotion*) Are you forgetting Him who died on Calvary? Are you forgetting the sorrow and terrible sadness of His Bloody Face as He looks at ye now? Will ye stand and watch each other draw the hard crooked thorns deep into His helpless body?
> (*backing towards door [as they become violent towards him]*)

Nothing in Heaven or Hell could move ye to see wrong!
> (*[as they come at him with a knife]*)

I'm going. You'll live to remember this night.

IRISH
MONOLOGUE
1M

THE PLAY:

Two actors play all the parts in this tragic-comedy set in a small Irish community. When a film begins shooting in their town, the locals are cast as extras, including the local "famous" extra, Mickey. But not everyone is included in the exciting (and lucrative) project. Young Sean Harkin was too messed up on drugs and alcohol to land a position on the film. As the cast and crew develop their own little society in the small town, Sean continues to feel more and more like an outcast. The tragic ending, and the meaning of the play's title, reveals the havoc wreaked on the small towns of Ireland when films come in and temporarily disrupt the lives of the locals . . . leaving permanent scars on the entire landscape.

THE MONOLOGUE:

Fin (late teens), Sean's best friend, tries to make Jake and the others understand why Sean was so out of sorts.

TIME & PLACE:

The wake. The Harkin farm. Evening.

FIN: Jake, everything he wanted was somewhere else . . . he hated this town. He said it let him down . . . everybody let him down . . . but sure that couldn't be helped . . . that's the way it was and nobody's fault . . . you know some of us just accepted that life wasn't great, but he wouldn't . . . he stopped going out he just got his gear and stayed in his room with his movies . . . virtual reality. That kept him going, drugs and movies.

He had tried to get on the movie the day before but he was out of his head . . . Then, that night in the pub . . . they were all there . . . . all arse lickin' the yanks it seemed he was right in the middle of the world he fantasised about . . . you know, the beautiful American star, the movies. He knew the crew had coke . . . they were all laughin' and joking and he just watched them and then he tried to score. He saw your woman talking to you and then he went up to her . . .

Enda Walsh

IRISH
MONOLOGUE
1 M

THE PLAY:

A man moves from County Cork to London with his two young sons. They live in a small apartment and rarely go out in public. When the play starts, we see the sons going through seemingly "normal" routines—unloading groceries, ironing clothes—but then the creepy and fascinating "farce" (play) really begins. Dinny (the father) makes his sons (Blake and Sean, now adults) *re-enact* the actions that led up to their leaving Ireland. Every last detail is replayed every single day. They eat the same meal, they say the same lines, and the ironed clothes (dresses) become their costumes as they play all the parts of every person in their family. On *this* day, however, something went wrong . . . the groceries were not the same. This small mistake sets the stage for a horrifying and haunting turn of events as the sons play their parts for the last time.

THE MONOLOGUE:

Blake (twenty-five) has just learned about the grocery mistake—no roast chicken tonight, it'll be cold salami—and it triggers his memory of his home country.

TIME & PLACE:

Present day. "A council flat on the Walworth Road, South London."Morning.

BLAKE: When we came here as little kids you could still smell Ireland from our jumpers. You could smell Mammy's cooking, couldn't you? It was roast chicken that last day and it was a lovely smell, hey Sean? And I think we might have come across on a boat . . . and I can't remember getting off a boat . . . but maybe we got a bus then to London, Sean, and still Mammy right around us. And for a while it stayed and we must have talked about the chicken smell and we must have missed Mammy, hey Sean?

Dad's all talk of Ireland, Sean. Everything's Ireland. His voice is stuck in Cork so it's impossible to forget what Cork is. *(a pause)* This story we play is everything. *(a pause)* Once upon a time my head was full of pictures of Granny's coffin and Mr. and Mrs. Cotter and Paddy and Vera and Bouncer the dog and all those busy pictures in our last day. *(Smiling)* 'Cause you'd say Dad's words and they'd give you pictures, wouldn't they, Sean? And so many pictures in your head . . . Sure you wouldn't want for the outside world even if it was a good world! You could be happy *(a pause)* But all them pictures have stopped. I say his words and all I can see is the word. A lot of words piled on top of other words. There's no sense to my day 'cause the sense isn't important anymore. No pictures. No dreams. Words only. *(a pause)* All I've got is the memory of the roast chicken, Sean.

THE WALWORTH FARCE

Enda Walsh

IRISH
MONOLOGUE
1 M

THE PLAY:

A man moves from County Cork to London with his two young sons. They live in a small apartment and rarely go out in public. When the play starts, we see the sons going through seemingly "normal" routines—unloading groceries, ironing clothes—but then the creepy and fascinating "farce" (play) really begins. Dinny (the father) makes his sons (Blake and Sean, now adults) *re-enact* the actions that led up to their leaving Ireland. Every last detail is replayed every single day. They eat the same meal, they say the same lines, and the ironed clothes (dresses) become their costumes as they play all the parts of every person in their family. On *this* day, however, something went wrong . . . the groceries were not the same. This small mistake sets the stage for a horrifying and haunting turn of events as the sons play their parts for the last time.

THE MONOLOGUE:

Sean (twenty-four) was so surprised that someone "on the outside" was actually kind to him and spoke to him, that he became distracted and picked up the wrong bag at the grocery store. As their scripted "farce" is thrown into improvisation by his mistake, he finds a moment to reveal to his brother what happened.

TIME & PLACE:

Present day. "A council flat on the Walworth Road, South London."Day.

GREAT MONOLOGUES IN DIALECT

SEAN: Well, today I spoke to someone. A girl in Tesco, Blake. Got all our food and paid her. She knows me 'cause I'm in at ten o'clock every morning getting the same food for the story. She says that she's seen where I live. Asks me what I do. I can't tell the truth of what we do in here all day so I say that I'm a builder, though I'm no builder. She's talked about Ireland and how she's seen it on the telly, Blake. She talks about the funny color of the grass and then the sea. I tell her that I like the sea but how I hadn't seen the sea in so long and she says, "I'll take you to Brighton Beach and we can walk there." She means it. She definitely means to take me to that place. So I leave sort of in a daze 'cause of the way she talked to me. I picked up the wrong shopping bag and didn't get out of the daze until I got back here and saw that fecking sausage. But her talking to me like that, Blake . . . even besides the great thing she said . . . her just talking so nice to me . . . it got me thinking more than ever . . . It's right that us two leave.

THE WALWORTH FARCE

Enda Walsh

IRISH
MONOLOGUE
1 M

THE PLAY:

A man moves from County Cork to London with his two young sons. They live in a small apartment and rarely go out in public. When the play starts, we see the sons going through seemingly "normal" routines—unloading groceries, ironing clothes—but then the creepy and fascinating "farce" (play) really begins. Dinny (the father) makes his sons (Blake and Sean, now adults) *re-enact* the actions that led up to their leaving Ireland. Every last detail is replayed every single day. They eat the same meal, they say the same lines, and the ironed clothes (dresses) become their costumes as they play all the parts of every person in their family. On *this* day, however, something went wrong . . . the groceries were not the same. This small mistake sets the stage for a horrifying and haunting turn of events as the sons play their parts for the last time.

THE MONOLOGUE:

Sean (twenty-four) has tried to keep the "farce" going in the regular fashion, but everything has conspired against him. As his father slowly loses his grip on the "story" they've been playing, Sean confronts him with what really happened on the day they left Ireland.

TIME & PLACE:

Present day. "A council flat on the Walworth Road, South London." Late afternoon/early evening.

SEAN: No, Dad. We're playing in our back garden me and Blake. Granny's coffin's open in the front room and the room smells of dust so you send us out into the fresh air. We're lying on the grass and we're talking about what we'll be when we're all grown up. Blake full of talk about being an astronaut. He's read a book on it and he knows some big words to do with space. He says he'd feel safe up there. He said if he got nervous he'd hide the earth behind his thumb. He talked about a parade in Dublin when the space men got back from space. How there'd have to be a special parade for him in Cork and everyone would come out and cheer him on and slag off the Dubs. We're just sitting on the grass chatting like that. *(a pause)* I say I want to be a bus driver because I like buses and Blake thinks that it's a great job. Just like driving a rocket 'cept your orbit's the Grand Parade and Mac Curtain Street. *(a pause)* There's shouting from inside the house. You and Uncle Paddy screaming at each other. Fighting over Granny's money even before she's stuck in the ground. Aunty Vera crying her cries real high like a baby crying. Your voice so much bigger than Uncle Paddy and him saying, "No, Dinny, no please, Dinny!" *(slight pause)* And then we hear Mammy screaming, Dad. We're both up fast and running through our back door and into our kitchen and the smell of the roast chicken. Her screaming coming from the sitting room and Blake won't go inside 'cause he's frightened of what he might see. But I do. I do go inside. And Mammy grabs me and spins me around fast so I can't see . . . but I see Uncle Paddy and Aunty Vera on the ground and I see you standing in the corner with blood all over your hands. There's blood on your hands and a kitchen knife, I'm sure of it. *(a pause)* Mam's terrible screaming. And you're standing at the door and I can see that you're trying to make up your mind whether to stay or to run. And Mammy kisses you and says "Leave now," and sets you free. You just step out to the outside and begin your run.

Latina/o

Unlike the British chapter and the Irish chapter which explained the dialect as being related to a geographic designation, the Latin-American dialect is not standard to a specific location nor a specific nationality of speaker. In fact, the term "Latina/o" has come to define a person who has Spanish or Portuguese (in Brazil) as an influential language in his/her life.

According to numerous websites and personal accounts, the exact definition of "Latino" or "Chicano" or "Hispanic" varies greatly depending on to whom you are speaking. From the perspective of a few of my colleagues, they consider themselves Latin because they are from, or their parents/ancestors are from Spanish speaking countries in South America, Central America, and Puerto Rico or Cuba. My Mexican friends consider themselves Mexican. More contemporary is the usage of the term "Chicano" to refer to Mexican-Americans. What is important to note is that a person of Latina/o heritage can be *of any race*. More important to the actor is to determine the character's historical and geographical background in order to establish which specific Latin-American sound changes they will incorporate.

With the presence of amazing Latino/Chicano plays and playwrights in the American theater scene (Nilo Cruz, Octavio Solis, Jose Rivera, Lynne Alvarez, Migdalia Cruz, Luis Alfaro . . . to name a few), there are many opportunities for actors to explore and use a "Latin-based" dialect.

As is true of all dialects, a person's country/language of origin is the primary factor in distinguishing the intricacies of the sound patterns, colloquial phrases and inflection variation. The education-level of the speaker, the amount of time spent out of the country of origin, and the need to remove or maintain a dialect also factor in to the strength of the speaker's sound. So the American actor playing a character with a Latino/a influence has many questions to ask. Does the person have Mexican lineage? Puerto Rican lineage? Have they been formally trained in English? Are they extensively well-traveled? Do they live in a predominantly Spanish neighborhood? What is their social class? What era is the play set?

Not all Latinos have strong dialects. The more recent the character's arrival to the U.S., the stronger the dialect tends to be. Also, if the person arrives and lives in a neighborhood where cultural identity is more than a source of pride, but also a source of protection, the dialect will remain strong but with "American" influences (note: the metropolitan areas of NYC).

Though the monologue selections represented here *can* be used with a Latina/o dialect, many of the plays are not done in dialect at all. Simply use the monologues as resources for practice and exposure to writing.

What follows are some basic and consistent sound changes that occur in the Latin American-based dialects.

These thoughts represent an amalgam of sounds from primarily South American, Cuban and Puerto Rican influences.

Sound/Music Thoughts:

● The rhythm of the Cuban accent resembles "the African drums" a staccato-type beat, according to one source. Edith Skinner describes it as a "lack of gliding from sound to sound."

● The pace of many Latina/o-English speakers is rapid. In some countries of South America, such as Argentina, the pace can be much slower.

● There is a tendency to stress the second to last syllable of a multi-syllabic word . . . i.e. " blockbuster" becomes "block BUS ter."

● Depending on the writing and your character's fluency, the new English speaker will usually neglect "small" words in sentences (articles, conjunctions, etc.).

● Occasionally, the Latino/a speaker will draw out a word and raise the inflection slightly at the end of the word to elicit a reaction from the listener.

Mouth/Physical Thoughts:

● In Cuba, the articulation of the sounds is relaxed and "casual," whereas in other regions of Latin America, there would be a formality to the pronunciation of both English and Spanish.

● There can be a tendency to slur the words a bit and to drop off the ends of the words or, occasionally, some of the consonants in the middle of words . . . doing this too often, or too authentically can pose a problem for your audience. Be careful.

Kimberly Mohne Hill   147

● Just as with any dialect, the more changes you do, the more stereotypical/exaggerated the dialect will sound. Be careful when choosing which elements to use, and then remember to always try to pronounce the word in its original form. In other words, if you work too hard at sounding "Latina/o" and forget about the character and the original intention of the line, you may sound cliché and untrue. Relax. Be the whole character - mind, body and voice.

LATIN-AMERICAN SOUND CHANGES

These sounds represent an amalgam of sounds from primarily South American, Cuban and Puerto Rican influences.

VOWEL CHANGES—A good rule of thumb for the vowels is to remember that the Spanish/English speaker will use the original Spanish vowel sounds for words that contain those letters in the spelling. There are only five pure vowel sounds in Spanish – a, e, i, o, u – pronounced (in Spanish) as "ah," "eh," "ee," "o," "oo."

[ih] → *[ee]*   *trip, pick, rich*   →   *treep, peek, reech*

[a] → *[ah]*   *back, that, man*   →   *bahck, daht, mahn*
(Intermediate 'a')

[u] → *[oo]*   *put, look, shouldn't*   →   *poot, look, shooden'*

[oh] → *[o:]*   *no, don't, ago*   →   *no:, do:n', ago:*
(Diphthong becomes one sound, [o] . . . not 'o' + 'u')

[ey] → *[e:]*   *they, make, play*   →   *de:, me:k, ple:*
(Diphthong becomes one sound, [e:] . . . not 'e' + 'i')

CONSONANT CHANGES

[r] trilled rrrate, brrrother, rrran, rrrubber, rrrock

[z]	→	*[s]*	*was, is, he's*	→ *wass, eess, he'ss*

[th] → *[t]/[s] nothing, something* → *noting/no'sing, someting/ so'sing*

[th] → *[d] this, that, mother* → *dees, deht, mudder*

[w] → *[hw] what, where, when, why*→ *hwat, hwere, hwen, hwy*

[h] extra air - hello, him, history, haircut

[n/m] → *[ng] him, home* → *heeng, hong*
(Final or medial position)

[t$_h$] → *[t$_1$ or d] not in, just in, shouldn't* → *nod in, jus' in, id shooden'*
(Drop the [t] or turn it into a [d])

[ks] → *[s] success, sixty, extreme* → *soosess, sisty, estreem*

Intrusive [eh] start, speak, spend → *$_h$star', $_{eh}$speek, $_{eh}$spen'*
(subtle, in newer English speakers)

Final consonants dropped:

couldn't, bite, like, warned → *cooden', by', ly', warn'*

ANTIQUATED/STEREOTYPICAL CHANGES – BE CAREFUL

[sh]	→	*[ch]*	*shape, ship, shoes*	→ *chehp, cheep, choos*
[zh]	→	*[sh]*	*rouge, treasure, pleasure*	→ *roushe, treashure, pleashure*
[y]	→	*[j]*	*you, yours, yes*	→ *joo, jours, jes*

[ih]   →   [ee]
If this is it, it didn't fit with his wish. The kid is the biggest wimp in history.

[a]   →   [ah]
Man, that band can't plan to stand in the back. Have manners, Andres.

[u]   →   [oo]
The book she took is good. Would you put the woman in the woods?

[ey]   →   [e:]
We may say which way to play the game. Stay to grade the papers, Ray.

[oh]   →   [o:]
Don't go to the road show, they'll know. They rowed the boat to go home.

[r]   →   rrr [trilled]
Around the rocks the rugged rascal ran. Run, Ricky, run and carry Lucy!

[z]   →   [s]
I was here because this is as it was. She does not like my cousin, Isabel.

[th]   →   [t]/[s]
Something tells me nothing is the same. Think about thanking me.

[th]   →   [d]/[z]
This is the other brother to the mother's third cousin. That is there!

[w]   →   [hw]
Why don't you ask where, or what or when anymore? Which is which?

[h] extra air
He is home with a hero's homecoming. History is here for her humour.

[n/m]   →   [ng]
The man said come to the welcome home from Spain party. My son is handsome.

[tʰ]   →   [t, or d]   (Drop the [t] or turn it into a [d])
It was a little bit of a hit on the head. Right after that one, it opened again.

[ks]   →   [s]
The success of the experiment is no accident. There's exactly sixty men.

Intrusive 'eh'
Speak Spanish and spread strong sentiments to Spain. Spring has sprung!

Final Consonants Dropped
She couldn't and she wouldn't because she didn't like being required to.

[sh]   →   [ch]
The show is in good shape. Shouldn't Sheila show the shiny shoes to the shoppers?

[zh]   →   [sh]
The vision is an illusion of pleasure. Treasure the beige rouge.

[y]   →   [j]
Yes, you are used to using your yellow pen. Yesterday, we went to Yale University.

LATIN-AMERICAN DIALECT SOUND SOURCES

INTERNET SOURCES:
    Internet sources can evolve and change over the years, so if any of the links below have expired, simply "Google search" the title of the link and you will be redirected to the updated site/location.

International Dialects of English Archive—www.dialectarchive.com
Speech Accent Archive—http://accent.gmu.edu/
StoryCorps – "Historias"—http://storycorps.org/historias-en/
Varieties of English—http://www.ic.arizona.edu/~lsp/index.html
"Voces Oral History Project"—http://www.lib.utexas.edu/voces/
PBS American Experience: The Zoot Suit Riots—http://www.pbs.org/wgbh/amex/zoot/
Library of Congress: American Folklife Center- Veteran's History Project – Hispanic
http://lcweb2.loc.gov/diglib/vhp/search?query=race:Hispanic

FILMS:
    (For a listing of many films with Latino characters/actors, see: Turner Classic Movies: Race & Hollywood, Latino Images in Films http://www.tcm.com/2009/lif/index.jsp)

Mi Familia	*Wrestling Hemingway*
Fidel	*La Bamba*
White Men Can't Jump	*The Motorcycle Diaries*
Stand and Deliver	*Kiss of the Spider Woman*
The Buena Vista Social Club	

TV:
    (While these shows may not be all Latino/a characters, there are characters on them that are Latino/a.)

Modern Family	*American Family*	*George Lopez*
CSI: Miami	*I Love Lucy*	*Alias*
Without a Trace		

CDS/COACHES:
Gillian Lane-Plescia—http://www.dialectresource.com/
AccentHelp—http://www.accenthelp.com/

LATINA MONOLOGUES

FEMALE

LATINA
MONOLOGUE
1 F

THE PLAY:

Set primarily in a cigar factory outside of Tampa, Florida (a small town called Ybor City), *Anna in the Tropics*, tells the story of a dying age in the history of America and factories. Where once there were cigar factories with workers who did everything by hand, including rolling the tobacco leaves into the cigars and putting the small cigar bands on them, the advancement of machinery signified both an exciting new age of possibility, and the end of an era. To entertain the workers, "lectors" were hired to read to the workers while they worked. The "Anna" in the title refers to *Anna Karenina*—the book the new lector chooses to read to the workers in the family cigar factory. The words of the story mirror the passions of the people in the factory, and we watch the tragic circumstances unfold almost as if we are seeing the world of Anna Karenina come to life in a new locale.

THE SCENE:

Conchita (thirty-two) is sensible, but not completely immune to the charms of the handsome and well-spoken Juan Julian. As he begins his tenure as the "lector," she begins to feel drawn to the romantic words of his novel, and the man reading them.

TIME & PLACE:

1929. Ybor City, Florida. Cigar factory. Daytime.

CONCHITA: I knew a fellow from New London. He was modest and reserved. So shy was this boy, that when he expressed any sort of feeling, he would excuse himself. *(laughs)* One day I gave him a braid that I'd cut from my hair and told him to bury it under a tree. I explained to him that back in the island most women cut their hair once a year on the 2nd of February, when plants and trees are pruned, for the feast of Saint Candelaria. I told him how women offer their hair to the earth and the trees, for all the greenery and fruits to come, and I gave him my little braid in a box and told him to choose a tree in the park.

And the boy looked at me with a strange face and said that he would feel embarrassed digging a hole in the middle of the park, in front of everybody. And that's when I took my braid back from him, took a shovel, dug a hole and put him to shame. From then on he never talked to me again. So he's the only person from New England that I've met.

LATINA
MONOLOGUE
1 F

THE PLAY:

Performed by three men playing multiple roles, *Bordertown* explores the history and relationship of the neighboring cities/countries of San Diego, California, USA and Tijuana, Mexico. Though written prior to 9/11 and the subsequent "border patrol" concerns, there are some scenes that are remarkably prescient. With humor, incredible character transformations, and regional "inside-jokes," Culture Clash manages to scrape beneath the surface of the race relations not only amongst the Caucasian San Diegans and Mexicans, but also among all new immigrants in this representation of a World Bordertown—revealing the universality of *identity* and *affiliation.*

THE MONOLOGUE:

A young girl, Julia (late teens), is a maid for a wealthy La Jolla woman. [La Jolla is the wealthy enclave of San Diego . . . much like the "Beverly Hills" of San Diego.] Here she details the circumstances of her arrival in the United States.

TIME & PLACE:

Here and now. She speaks to the audience.

JULIA: To cross the border is a big decision, it's like being reborn. I never walk so much in my life. Two days to cross. Not just one mountain, but mountain after mountain. In the day I was so hot and thirsty, it hurt to swallow. At night I was so scared. I couldn't see in front of me and I kept falling down. My feet were bleeding. I had to keep up with the men. And it was so cold, I couldn't stop shaking. We almost make it, but they catch us. And they were so rough; they pull out guns; they push us and call us bad names. They deport us back to Mexicali.

We called our Mama. She live in San Diego. We cry to her on the telephone. She say to us, no try to cross again. But the next day we try again, again it took two days, more walking, all those mountains, six miles of mountains, but this time we make it across! Cruzamos el cerco. I never forget the look on my mama's face when we surprise her. We hug and cry. I'll never forget that day, it was my quinceanera, my fifteen-year birthday.

We not know anyone here in San Diego. But we meet a group that help and accept us. They made us feel wanted here. We join the Mormons. Dios mio, it was so funny when we got baptized! My brothers, sisters, y Mama, all of us dressed in white. We looked like angels. We had to hold our laughter. We were reborn. You know that big white Mormon temple, the one in La Jolla, the one that looks like a spaceship? One day they let us go inside.

LATINA
MONOLOGUE
1 F

THE PLAY:

Ten-year-old Sasha, the daughter of a hard-working Russian immigrant, has been having a tough time starting her research paper about the Brooklyn Bridge. As the deadline looms, she breaks her mother's number one rule and leaves her apartment in search of a pen. Instead, she finds friendship and support from her eclectic neighbors.

THE MONOLOGUE:

Talidia (a mother with lots of laundry) gives Sasha some words of advice and encouragement as the two wait on the front stoop of their building for someone to let them back inside.

TIME & PLACE:

The front stoop of Sasha and Talidia's apartment building. Brooklyn . . . in the shadows of the Brooklyn Bridge. Present day. Around 7 pm.

TALIDIA: Listen
I don't know your father
I don't know your mother
I don't know you
But I do know that the other thing about people who aren't

here
is that they lose their shape
Some become huge
Some become tiny
None resemble what they really are
What I'm saying is you can't trust what people's absences
turn them into
One funny-but-not-so-funny thing is that your mother's
not here
because she working so YOU can be here
in this apartment building
in this country
in this other life that she wants you to have
Another funny-but-not-so funny thing is that your father's
not here
but his words are
thousands and thousands of them
because for whatever reason they are all he has to give you
right now
Does it matter what those words are
I don't know
You have to decide
But I do know
that parents are exactly who they are
and even if they are not enough
they are what you have
You're not supposed to have to deal with such a fact at
your age
But for whatever reason life constantly asks us to deal with
all sorts
of age-inappropriate things
(slight pause)
Wait
There's one last thing I know
whatever your mother and father aren't able to do or be
whatever it is that you need that they can't give you
you must find it somewhere else
because it exists somewhere else
because everything we need exists somewhere
We just have to find where

Kimberly Mohne Hill   159

LATINA
MONOLOGUE
1 F

THE PLAY:
Bill is a successful car dealership owner, the husband of a beautiful wife, and the father of two children. Sublimating his ancient despair over having to step into the exact same life that his father lived has led Bill to be a grumpy, unhappy, careless man who gets no respect from anyone in his near circle and who drives the people he cares about away with his callousness. When his wife can no longer bear his refusal to confront his unrest, she leaves him and he is shocked into realizing what he has been feeling all along. This "awakening" takes place as he embarks on a road trip across the country to Albuquerque with his secretary, Naranja, the only person who still seems to like him. Though his original goal was to get his wife back, he returns to Fresno having only gained new appreciation for his father, a new "salesman" (Naranja) and a new outlook on his life.

THE MONOLOGUE:
Naranja (early twenties) has accompanied her boss on his quest to find his wife. As they prepare to rest at a hotel for the night, she reveals her secret desire . . . to be a "salesman" at the dealership he own, not just his secretary anymore. Bill gives her the opportunity to "audition" for the part by trying out her sales pitch.

TIME & PLACE:
Spring 2001. A motel room near Albuquerque, New Mexico. Late morning, early afternoon.

NARANJA: (practicing her "sales-pitch" to her boss, Bill) Do you . . . do you like this model?

[Bill: Yeah, sure, whatever.]

No whatever, sir. I tell you secret, you not tell anybody. The Park Avenue is easily my favorite model of all the cars on the lot. Do you know why? I bet you know what I am thinking . . .

It is the strongest-looking of all the cars on the lot. It has style. People, they often say, Buicks, not a stylish car. But this model—I think it really has a flair. And you would look exceptional driving it. You would look . . . strong.

Absolutely. And it is not just that it has this style. I feel it is the car which is right for you. Let me tell you why. Power and comfort. This is what the Park Avenue has. Power. Comfort. I see that you are a man who need the extra horse-power you can only get with the special supercharged V-6 engine that come with the Park Avenue. You would like to have that little extra kick, yes, who would not?

But you also need the extra comfort—the extra luxury of the Park Avenue. Ten-way power front seats—you, as you should—would have absolute control. This feature only comes in our Park Avenue. Also available in our Ultra package, only in the Park Avenue, are heated front seats with lumbar adjustment. You and your lovely wife—what is your wife's name?

[Bill: Millicent]

You and Millicent are taking a long drive on a beautiful chilly winter night. It is romantic. You feel in control of the road with your four-speed automatic transmission, your antilock four-wheel disc brakes, your supercharged 3.8 liter V-6 engine. You and your wife are comfortable. But you are . . . a little cold. And your back is a little stiff. You are a tall man. You need space for breathing. In the Park Avenue, you have the highest combination of front leg room and head of any of our spacious Buick models. You would ride in great comfort, with great power at your fingertips. The Ultra package, which I am sure you would be interested in, goes for merely thirty-eight thousand one hundred dollars. I think one test drive will suffice to show you that the Buick Park Avenue is the best car for you. Shall we take spin, or wait for your lovely wife, Millicent?

LATINA
MONOLOGUE
1 F

THE PLAY:

Bill is a successful car dealership owner, the husband of a beautiful wife, and the father of two children. Sublimating his ancient despair over having to step into the exact same life that his father lived has led Bill to be a grumpy, unhappy, careless man who gets no respect from anyone in his near circle and who drives the people he cares about away with his callousness. When his wife can no longer bear his refusal to confront his unrest, she leaves him and he is shocked into realizing what he has been feeling all along. This "awakening" takes place as he embarks on a road trip across the country to Albuquerque with his secretary, Naranja, the only person who still seems to like him. Though his original goal was to get his wife back, he returns to Fresno having only gained new appreciation for his father, a new "salesman" (Naranja) and a new outlook on his life.

THE MONOLOGUE:

Naranja (early twenties) has accompanied her boss on his quest to find his wife. As they prepare to rest at a hotel for the night, she reveals her secret desire . . . to be a "salesman" at the dealership he own, not just his secretary anymore. Bill gives her the opportunity to "audition" for the part by trying out her sales pitch. After the audition, she gives Bill a little bit of history as to why she feels "credentialed" to be a salesman.

TIME & PLACE:

Spring 2001. A motel room near Albuquerque, New Mexico. Late morning, early afternoon.

NARANJA: *(after her sales-pitch to her boss, Bill)* So you are giving me job?

Do not make funny of me! You give me advice. Why give me advice if you not giving me job! Do not make funny of me!

I am doing you a favor! You need new business, same people always come in.

Look like same people. You need a little color. Expand business. Sell some Mexican people cars.

I have been in sales. I work in big tourist hotel. At front desk. It is sales. People come from all over world, I must make things OK, make them still think is good hotel even if we mess things up. I work in Manzanillo, it is major tourist destination, there are many other hotels, they go somewhere else. This is sales!

There is this one time this Swedish man come to hotel. He have terrible trip. His luggage lost, he get wallet stolen at airport, he get sick from his airplane food0151he is not happy. He come to hotel and his room is not available, somebody mess up. He must get smaller room. I never see someone so angry and so sad. But I take him up to room, I show him it is nice room. I make him feel OK, about the room. He like everything in it. This—I sell him.

I work at one of the best hotels in all of Manzanillo. It is very glamorous, it is right at the beach. It is really so beautiful right there on the beach. The rest of town, it is just Mexico, but the ocean and the beach . . . And the job, I am lucky to have it, everybody keep telling me. It is not easy job, but I am good at it. At selling to all these people who come from all over, to my little corner of the world. At making things be OK for them. Even when I do not want to. But this—this is why I think maybe I can sell cars, like you!

LATINA
MONOLOGUE
1 F

THE PLAY:

Bill is a successful car dealership owner, the husband of a beautiful wife, and the father of two children. Sublimating his ancient despair over having to step into the exact same life that his father lived has led Bill to be a grumpy, unhappy, careless man who gets no respect from anyone in his near circle and who drives the people he cares about away with his callousness. When his wife can no longer bear his refusal to confront his unrest, she leaves him and he is shocked into realizing what he has been feeling all along. This "awakening" takes place as he embarks on a road trip across the country to Albuquerque with his secretary, Naranja, the only person who still seems to like him. Though his original goal was to get his wife back, he returns to Fresno having only gained new appreciation for his father, a new "salesman" (Naranja) and a new outlook on his life.

THE MONOLOGUE:

Naranja (early twenties) has accompanied her boss on his quest to find his wife. They found out that she wasn't in Albuquerque . . . that she really doesn't want him to find her. On their way back to Fresno, Bill stops at a bar and gets mugged/beaten by a stranger. As Naranja tends to him, they make love. Afterwards, Bill believes she slept with him just to get the job.

[Note: this monologue contains strong language]

TIME & PLACE:

Spring 2001. A motel room in a small southwest town. Late night. After they have made love.

NARANJA: *(to Bill)* No, I am a salesman. My job was to make everything always OK. I am selling everything. You remember, I tell you about the customer from Sweden?

I thought you want to hear all about my life, but you do not even listen. I help him, I am very helpful to him, I make him feel better after he has such a hard trip to Mexico. And he is grateful, he is so grateful, he take my arm and pull me next to him and he kiss me and when I tell him to stop he say the manager tell him "Whatever I wanted with the room" and that I know what this mean, and he kiss me again. He think I am going to fuck him, that I am a little extra. That I am part of the deal. I tell the hotel manager. The manager, he pretend he is shocked. He say, "You poor girl." He say, "You do not do this thing, yes?" But I look at him, and he is not minding so much. He is glad the man from Sweden is staying at his hotel. That he is enjoying his stay in Manzanillo, Mexico, in our lovely country. He does not care whether I fuck him or not.

No one thinks it would be a bad idea if I did. Not the manager, not the other girls at the front desk, no one. But this is not what I want to do, who I want to be. Who I am. So I come here, I start fresh. I am far away from there.

At least I think I am.

LATINA
MONOLOGUE
1 F

THE PLAY:

The subtitle, "a Chicano Take on the Tragedy of Electra," reveals the nature of the body of the play. The Greek tragedy is retold in a contemporary, "East Side" (L.A.) city location with the world of the cholo gang providing a place for "the king" to rule. When he is killed by his wife, his eldest daughter, Electricidad, removes his body from the funeral home and sets it on her own altar in her front yard. She proceeds to spend all day and night mourning him out in the open, loudly for all to see and hear – much to the dismay of her mother and grandmother. The Greek Chorus is recast as a group of gossiping "vecinas" (neighbors). In true Greek tragedy form, the long-lost hope for the barrio (neighborhood), Orestes, Electricidad's brother, returns at the end of the play to provide the gruesome, tragic ending.

THE MONOLOGUE:

Electricidad (twenty-three) calls up to her father as she continues in her process of mourning and protest.

TIME & PLACE:

Present. Morning. Near enough to the freeways to be able to hear them in the distance. The front "yarda" of Electricidad's house at the end of the block. In front of the altar made of stones. The rest of the yard is dirt and shrubs and stones "and some stuff that doesn't fit in the house."

ELECTRICIDAD: Papa?

Why do I keep looking up to see heaven, but I only get as far as the sky?

Why is it the only light that shines on me is the happy face of the helicopter?

I wonder if you could be born again and really come back?

I am waiting for a cloud to pass by and spit in my mouth.

But the Santa Anas keep pushing them away.

To Vegas, I guess . . .

But I can wait.

When I finally get god to spit down on me, I am going to say that it is a blessing and I am going to use my spit to gritar my sorrow, and my rage, and my anger and all the other injusticias.

I don't care how I sound.

I don't care what they think.

I will free you, Papa.

From your death.

I will do that.

I don't know how yet, but I will do it.

LATINA
MONOLOGUE
1 F

THE PLAY:

The subtitle, "a Chicano Take on the Tragedy of Electra," reveals the nature of the body of the play. The Greek tragedy is retold in a contemporary, "East Side" (L.A.) city location with the world of the cholo gang providing a place for "the king" to rule. When he is killed by his wife, his eldest daughter, Electricidad, removes his body from the funeral home and sets it on her own altar in her front yard. She proceeds to spend all day and night mourning him out in the open, loudly for all to see and hear – much to the dismay of her mother and grandmother. The Greek Chorus is recast as a group of gossiping "vecinas" (neighbors). In true Greek tragedy form, the long-lost hope for the barrio (neighborhood), Orestes, Electricidad's brother, returns at the end of the play to provide the gruesome, tragic ending.

THE MONOLOGUE:

After another confrontation with her mother, Electricidad's (twenty-three) passion for revenge is reunited. She talks to her father's body loudly enough for her mother to hear her as she strengthens her anger, passion, and resolve for revenge.

TIME & PLACE:

Present. Still morning. Near enough to the freeways to be able to hear them in the distance. The front "yarda" of Electricidad's house at the end of the block. In front of the altar made of stones. The rest of the yard is dirt and shrubs and stones "and some stuff that doesn't fit in the house."

SPANISH TRANSLATIONS:
  "mujer" = *woman*
  "comida" = *food*

"vieja" = old lady
"carniceria" = butcher
"veterano" = veteran
"pero a mi no me importa" = I don't care
"y la muerte" = and the death
"vecinas .tambien" = neighbors . . . also
"energia" = energy
"cervezas" = beers
"razon" = reason

ELECTRICIDAD: Did you hear her, Papa?
> *(she spits towards the house)*

See? She doesn't mourn you. La noche of your funeral, she put on the K-Earth 101 and served tamales and wine coolers. I didn't even know she could cook!
> *(beat—looks at him and realizes)*

Ai, Papa, I'm sorry. All this talking makes you tired. You are a man of so few words . . . But I must tell the stories you told me. About who we are and where we came from. Or I will forget.

We were Aztecas, huh, Papa?

And the mujer god of human sacrifices, Coatlicue, made the first cholo.

And she gave the first cholo the switchblade, so that he could leave the barrio and defend himself.

And then she gave the cholo some baggy pants, so that he could store the comida he shoplifted from the 7-Eleven.

And then she gave him Art Laboe and the oldies and taught him how to dance.

(she dances slow, cholo style, in the yarda)

And then she gave the cholos house parties and Schlitz, to make them happy.

And she gave them the lowrider and car club, so that they could show off to one another.

And finally she gave them the boulevard, so that they could cruise and see how beautiful they were . . . *(stops dancing)*

But then, one of her four hundred daughters, Coyolxauqui, stood up to her and was like, "Why you get all the power, vieja? Why you get to decide everything for us?"

And that's when Coatlicue cut her up in four, carniceria

Kimberly Mohne Hill 169

style, and made the four corners cholo world.

First corner—North Side Locos, control Adelphia cable.

Second corner—South Side Locos, control Vernon slaughterhouses.

Third corner—West Side Locos, got all the bail bonds.

And fourth corner—us, the East Side Locos, control neighborhood pride and "pharmacy" traffic.

And then she cut her daughter's head off and did a fly ball into the sky, and her head became the moon.

And that's the one I'm trying to see every night, Papa.

But she won't show me her expressions.

She's a stone-cold chola, that daughter.

And since the beginning of cholo time, this is how it was and always will be.

But someone wants to change that.

Oh, you know who I'm talking about.

She says it's progress. She thought that if she killed you, all the ways of the cholo would end. But she was wrong, because all she did was offend the Council of Old Cholos. Who never forget.

That's why I must say your name, Papa.

Or it will lose its power.

I must yell your name out loud or I will forget it, Papa.

> *(she yells out to the barrio as if she is calling him back from the dead)*

AGAMEMNON ATRIDAS . . . . .

VETERANO . . . . .

DE LOS EAST SIDE LOCOS . . .

Everyday I will scream your name.

And they will get tired of hearing it and of hearing me.

(yells to the house)

PERO A MI NO ME IMPORTA!

(leans in to his body as if telling him a secret)

I am going to avenge your death.

Y la muerte of our sweetest and gentlest Orestes.

I will turn Ifigenia, my so-called sister, against her.

I will turn the vecinas against her, tambien.

Oh Papa, it is only in the thought of her suffering that I get my energia.

Thinking of her lifeless body thrown at the doorway of El Gato Negro bar. *(laughs at the joy of seeing such an image)* The drunks stepping on her as they reach for their cervezas.

Yes, I have a razon to live!

(yells)

AGAMEMNON ATRIDAS . . .

VETERANO . . .

DE LOS EAST SIDE LOCOS . . .

Oh yes, I would do anything to trade your death with my breath.

LATINA
MONOLOGUE
1 F

THE PLAY:

Veronica's wealthy parents fled to the United States when the Communist Revolution overtook Cuba. Staying behind with her husband, a former employee of her father's, Veronica embraces the revolution and all it promises. Her husband is rewarded for their loyalty with a position in the government. Though deeply enthusiastic and optimistic about the new regime and the positive changes it would bring to the society and the roles of all people (namely, women), Veronica soon learns exactly what her new role in this revolutionary society will be . . . at a cost she never expected.

THE MONOLOGUE:

Veronica (early twenties) is passionate about the changes that the communist revolution and Fidel Castro promised to bring to the people of Cuba. She even refused to follow her wealthy family to America, choosing instead to stay behind with her father's former bellboy, her new husband. Here, she reads from a book which had a significant influence on her as a young girl.

TIME & PLACE:

Early evening. December 1960. A large house in Havana, Cuba—Veronica's father's mansion. The library/den/living room area.

VERONICA: I want my life to start. *(looking at one of the books)* Proust. I loved Proust growing up.

> *(she puts down the book and walks over to one of the bookshelves. She gets a book.)*

Here it is. My father's copy. He gave it to me when I turned fifteen. Listen.

> *(Veronica reads)*

"But for me it was enough if, in my own bed, my sleep was so heavy as completely to relax my consciousness; for then I lost all sense of the place in which I had gone to sleep, and when I awoke at midnight, not knowing where I was, I could not be sure at first who I was; I had only the most rudimentary sense of existence, such as may lurk and flicker in the depths of an animal's consciousness; I was more destitute of human qualities than the cave-dweller; but then the memory, not yet of the place in which I was, but of various other places where I had lived, and might now very possibly be, would come like a rope let down from heaven to draw me up out of the abyss of not-being, from which I could never have escaped by myself . . ."

> *(she looks up at Manuel)*

All of a sudden I miss home.

LATINA
MONOLOGUE
1 F

THE PLAY:

Veronica's wealthy parents fled to the United States when the Communist Revolution overtook Cuba. Staying behind with her husband, a former employee of her father's, Veronica embraces the revolution and all it promises. Her husband is rewarded for their loyalty with a position in the government. Though deeply enthusiastic and optimistic about the new regime and the positive changes it would bring to the society and the roles of all people (namely, women), Veronica soon learns exactly what her new role in this revolutionary society will be . . . at a cost she never expected.

THE MONOLOGUE:

Veronica (early twenties) is passionate about the changes that the communist revolution and Fidel Castro promised to bring to the people of Cuba. After learning that she would have to sleep with the Associate Minister of Culture (Pepin) in order for her husband to advance any further in the government, she begins the affair—considering it her duty to her husband and her country. Here, she reminisces with Pepin about the way it used to be in her home.

TIME & PLACE:

December 1960. Havana, Cuba. Veronica's father's mansion. The reading room. Daytime/Mid-Day.

VERONICA: (*to Pepin*) Do you ever get—do you remember things from your past. Things you had forgotten. Like a painting has the—to remember what you were like. It happens sometimes when I'm alone. I go into my older sister's room—she has this little music box that I open and Schumann plays. And just as it gets—I think she's going to walk through the door. I wait and I wait but she never comes back.

I've spent my whole life in this house. Do you think they have similar memories? My sisters. Do they remember? It takes one hundred and eighty-six steps from my room to the front of the house—that is if you cut across the patio. I just did that again the other day. We used to do that. When we were learning to count. We'd spend all day counting steps. Do they remember that?

Luis Valdez

LATINA
MONOLOGUE
1 F

THE PLAY:

Spiritual, mystical, musical and symbolic combine with modern realism to tell the story of Mama Chu—an elderly Mexican Revolutionary with a sordid and mysterious past. When she lies in the hospital, comatose, her family gathers from all parts of the country to bid their farewells. Only Armida, her granddaughter, seems to want her to live . . . if only to finally clear up the mystery surrounding her roots. Who was her father? Why did her mother kill herself? How did Mama Chu outlast every single one of her husbands? The pain that brought Mama to the hospital has a profound meaning in the lives of her whole family—it's as if Mama's secret could no longer be held inside her.

THE MONOLOGUE:

Armida (twenties) comes back from Berkeley to visit Mama Chu in the hospital. Militant and angry, she is not content to let her grandmother die without a fight. Here, she visits her for the first time.

TIME & PLACE:

San Diego, California. 1969. Spring. A hospital room. Night time.

ARMIDA: *(stunned by the stillness of her grandmother . . .*
Suddenly awkward) Mama Chu . . . can you hear me? It's
me, Armida. Your . . . heartbreaker, remember? Well, I'm
back! I've been away a long time, I know, but even if you
haven't heard from me lately . . . I swear . . . I've missed
you, grandma. Are you still mad at me? I've been doing a
lot of thinking. I'm sorry, okay . . . I didn't even know who
I was till I left. I've changed, Mama Chu. Please don't give
me the silent treatment. I know you can hear me, Mama
Chu. Go ahead, let her rip. *Get-your-Yaqui-up!* I'm here.
Be pissed at me, I don't care. I can take it. We've got too
much to talk about. Can you hear me, Mama Chu? You've
got to fight this!

(Nurse reappears in the doorway)
What have you done to her?

LATINA
MONOLOGUE
1 F

THE PLAY:

The Soviet Union has collapsed, the "Iron Curtain" has come down and ideas like "Perestroika" have begun to take root in the newly free societies. In Cuba, however, two sisters are released from prison only to remain under house arrest in their once-grand, now stark and utilitarian home. A piano remains the only reminder of their former lives—lives filled with music and literature and warmth and color, now turned to empty shells of memory and fast-fading hope. When the Lieutenant assigned to monitor the women arrives on the scene, the highly controlled lives of the three begin to swirl out of control—at least briefly—until, eventually, the cruel order is restored and the women are left with nothing.

THE MONOLOGUE:

Forbidden from writing her novels after she signed a petition in support of Perestroika, Maria Celia (thirty-six) now composes her stories in her head. Also leery of the regime's tight control over the mail and any communication leaving the country, she has to "write" to her husband in her mind and send him her thoughts. As the play opens, we hear her composing her love letter to her husband and sending it to him in the distance.

TIME & PLACE:

The roof top of Maria Celia's house. Cuba. 1991. Morning.

MARIA CELIA: "Antonio, my dear husband, I'm standing on top of this roof, wanting to leap into the sky and send you this letter. Almost three months and two weeks now and not a word from you. Today a few militia guards came to search the house. They took inventory of all our things. I don't know what this means. This is usually done when somebody is leaving the country. Yesterday we heard on the radio about amnesty for political prisoners, so I'm keeping my fingers crossed. I tell Sofie that 1991 is our lucky year. We've been allowed back home. At least here we can walk all the way from the kitchen to the living room, and that's a long distance compared to the size of our cell back in prison. It seems that there are so many things happening out there in the world, my love . . . A new way of thinking . . . Freedom . . . I always tell Sofie how much I love the leader Gorbachev (any man who has a birthmark that looks like an island on his forehead is a blessed man). I'm writing a new story, my love, which I'm sending you a page at a time. It's what keeps me going. The writing. The man and the woman in my new story, they take me out of this house. Their walks to the sea. I miss you more and more, my love. A big kiss and a hug, Maria Celia."

LATINA
MONOLOGUE
1 F

THE PLAY:

An American classic, *Zoot Suit* re-tells in poetic theatricality the story of the famous L.A. "Zoot Suit Riots" of 1942-43. With historical details and characters and a guiding "Pachuco" helping the narration along, we follow the story of Henry Reyna as he and his friends endure false imprisonment under court-sanctioned World War II racism. After a lengthy trial and many moments of judicial misconduct by the judge, the boys were convicted of the crime and sent to San Quentin. A massive effort by the community to repeal the conviction ended with the eventual release of all the men.

THE MONOLOGUE:

Della (twenty) appears to testify in court on behalf of her boyfriend, Henry Reyna.

TIME & PLACE:

L.A. County Courthouse. October, 1942. Morning.

DELLA: That's when we heard music coming from the Williams' Ranch again. We didn't know Rafas and his gang had been there too, causing trouble. So when Joey said . . . . [*Hey there's a party! Bertha, let's crash it!*] We all went up there yelling and laughing. At the Williams' Ranch they saw us coming and thought we were the Downey Gang coming back again . . . They attacked us. An old man ran out of the house with a kitchen knife and Henry had to hit him. Then a girl grabbed me by the hair and in a second everybody was fighting! People were grabbing sticks from the fence, bottles, anything! It all happened so fast, we didn't know what hit us, but Henry said let's go!

And we started to back off . . . Before we got to the cars, I saw something out of the corner of my eye . . . it was a guy. He was hitting a man on the ground with a big stick. Henry called to him, but he wouldn't stop. He wouldn't stop . . . He wouldn't stop . . . He wouldn't stop . . . *(Della in tears . . .)*

Driving back in the car, everybody was quiet, like nothing had happened. We didn't know Jose Williams had died at the party that night and that the guys would be arrested the next day for murder.

LATINO MONOLOGUES

MALE

ADORATION OF THE OLD WOMAN

Jose Rivera

LATINO
MONOLOGUE
1 M

THE PLAY:

As Puerto Rico faces a future of American statehood an old woman, Belen, is haunted by her past. The ghost of her husband's lover, Adoración, shares her bed . . . the bed where Belen miscarried every single one of her seven babies. She is also regularly visited by her two "sons," Cheo and Israel, who stand on opposite sides of the statehood debate. They agree on one thing: Belen's visiting "great-granddaughter," Vanessa, is beautiful and fascinating and they both seek to woo her to themselves and their cause. Vanessa's heart is won by Cheo, even as Cheo's side loses the political debate. Meanwhile, Belen is finally dying (she is almost 150 years old), but she must first confront Adoración and admit the truth of why she is haunted. She let Adoración die giving birth to Belen's husband's baby . . . a baby Belen then raised as her own. When Vanessa figures it out, Belen is free to let go and leave the world of the living. Adoración gently walks with Belen into the "next life" as Puerto Rico prepares to do the same.

THE MONOLOGUE:

Cheo (twenty-six) has a personal, emotional reason for rejecting the US proposition of statehood. He truly believes that Puerto Rico could survive and thrive without the money and influence of the US because he remembers what it used to be like *before* US money entered the Puerto Rican scene. Here, he begins to confide in Vanessa.

TIME & PLACE:

The front porch of Dõna Belen's "one bedroom concrete house in rural, near-future Puerto Rico."Sunset. January 6.

CHEO: *(to Vanessa)* When you're in Puerto Rico, you should take a real good look around. Before it's too late. And don't do it with Izzy—he only knows what the tourists know. Promise me you'll do that? Because all this is gonna be gone some day. Little neighborhoods like Las Arenas, their little plots of land, full of chickens and pigs, this semi-independent way of life . . . it's all disappearing, like the coqui..getting buried . . . as the highways get closer. Even the stories told by old women like Doña Belen, the stories that hold these barrios together and connect the past with the present . . . all that's dying.

(looks at her, wondering how much he can confide)
There was a place I used to swim in , when I was a kid. On the beach, outside Arecibo, beautiful little bay called La Posa. It was my spot. Diving off the rocks. Time would stop for us. Black kids, white kids, we were one color: the color of fish. And the ocean was our home. The sun was our clock. Nobody was hungry in that water. Nobody was ignorant. I used to think . . . it must've been like this for the Tainos: perfect, pure, endless. One day I walked there . . . there's a fence. La Posa was bought by a US hotel chain and the thing that was mine—and all us kids—was out of reach. For the fucking rich tourists.

I hated that fence. Made my hands and feet bloody trying to do Kung-Fu on it. Begged Doña Belen to hit it with a curse. But La Posa died. When I stopped breaking my hands, I went home to think and I realized the only way out of this was nonviolent political action. That's all I've thought about. Now I'm a month away from finding out if I wasted my life.

I think I know my people, Vanessa. And we're so damn *restless*, so ready for a new concept of home, we're on the verge of exploding! Something's going to be born next month. The question is what.

Nilo Cruz

LATINO
MONOLOGUE
1 M

THE PLAY:
    Set primarily in a cigar factory outside of Tampa, Florida (a small town called Ybor City), *Anna in the Tropics*, tells the story of a dying age in the history of America and factories. Where once there were cigar factories with workers who did everything by hand, including rolling the tobacco leaves into the cigars and putting the small cigar bands on them, the advancement of machinery signified both an exciting new age of possibility, and the end of an era. To entertain the workers, "lectors" were hired to read to the workers while they worked. The "Anna" in the title refers to *Anna Karenina*—the book the new lector chooses to read to the workers in the family cigar factory. The words of the story mirror the passions of the people in the factory, and we watch the tragic circumstances unfold almost as if we are seeing the world of Anna Karenina come to life in a new locale.

THE SCENE:
    Juan Julian (thirty-eight) is the lector at the cigar factory. He begins to develop an affinity for one of the workers, Conchita, as they share personal stories.

TIME & PLACE:
    1929. Ybor City, Florida. Cigar factory. Daytime.

JUAN JULIAN: I don't really like cities. In the country one has freedom. When I'm in a city I feel asphyxiated. I feel constriction in my lungs. The air feels thick and dense, as if the buildings breathe and steal away the oxygen. As my father used to say, living in a city is like living inside the mouth of a crocodile, buildings all around you like teeth. The teeth of culture, the mouth and tongue of civilization. It's a silly comparison, but it makes sense to me.

Every time I go to a park, I'm reminded of how we always go back to nature. We build streets and buildings. We work five to six days a week, building and cementing our paths and down come tumbling trees and nests, a whole paradise of insects. And all for what? On Sundays we return to a park where we could still find greenery. The verdure of nature.

I discovered books one summer. My father owed a lot of money to a creditor and we had to close ourselves up in our house and hide for a while. For my family, keeping up appearances was important. We had to pretend that we had gone away on a trip. We told neighbors that my mother was ill and she had to recuperate somewhere else. We stayed in that closed-up house for more than two months, while my father worked abroad. I remember it was hot and all the windows were kept closed. The heat was unbearable. The maid was the only one who went out to buy groceries. And while being closed up in our own home my mother read books to the family. And that's when I became a listener and I learned to appreciate stories and the sound of words.

LATINO
MONOLOGUE
1 M

THE PLAY:

Set primarily in a cigar factory outside of Tampa, Florida (a small town called Ybor City), *Anna in the Tropics*, tells the story of a dying age in the history of America and factories. Where once there were cigar factories with workers who did everything by hand, including rolling the tobacco leaves into the cigars and putting the small cigar bands on them, the advancement of machinery signified both an exciting new age of possibility, and the end of an era. To entertain the workers, "lectors" were hired to read to the workers while they worked. The "Anna" in the title refers to *Anna Karenina*—the book the new lector chooses to read to the workers in the family cigar factory. The words of the story mirror the passions of the people in the factory, and we watch the tragic circumstances unfold almost as if we are seeing the world of Anna Karenina come to life in a new locale.

THE SCENE:

Juan Julian (thirty-eight) has endeared himself to the workers of the factory—considering himself almost a part of the fabric of the factory work-force and not simply "the entertainment."Here, he tries to rally the workers to reject the advancement of machinery, which, though cost-effective, would ultimately put the workers out of work . . . himself included.

TIME & PLACE:

1929. Ybor City, Florida. Cigar factory. Daytime.

JUAN JULIAN: Senor Chester, allow me to say something. My father used to say that the tradition of having readers in the factories goes back to the Taino Indians. He used to say that tobacco leaves whisper the language of the sky. And that's because through the language of the cigar smoke the Indians used to communicate to the gods. Obviously I'm not an Indian, but as a lector I am a distant relative of the Cacique, the Chief Indian, who used to translate the sacred words of the deities. The workers are the oidores. The ones who listen quietly, the same way the Taino Indians used to listen. And this is the tradition that you're trying to destroy with your machine. Instead of promoting and popularizing machines, why don't you advertize our cigars? Or are you working for the machine industry? Let's face it, Chester, workers, cigars are not popular anymore. Moving pictures now feature their stars smoking cigarettes: Valentino, Douglas Fairbanks . . . They are all smoking little fags and not cigars. You can go to Hollywood and offer our cigars to producers.

I'm warning you. This fast mode of living with machines and moving cars affects cigar consumption. And do you want to know why, Senor Chester? Because people prefer a quick smoke, the kind you get from a cigarette. The truth is that machines, cars, are keeping us from taking walks and sitting on park benches, smoking a cigar slowly and calmly. The way they should be smoked. So you see, Chester, you want modernity, and modernity is actually destroying our very own industry. The very act of smoking a cigar.

I can certainly step out of the room if you want to take a vote.

LATINO
MONOLOGUE
1 M

THE PLAY:

On the eve of her Quinceañera (her fifteenth birthday), Ceci was thrown through the windshield of the car her brother was driving. It left her in a paralytic, nearly vegetative state. Her bed is in the front room of the house so she can be constantly cared for by her family. When her mother hires a new immigrant worker, Lydia, to care for her, their immediate bond is magical. Some of the pressure the family has endured releases, and some of it rises back up to the surface—especially with the arrival of their cousin, Alvaro, freshly back from Vietnam and now working for the Border Patrol. Through lyrical, mystical staging and storytelling, the circumstances of Ceci's accident are brought to the forefront before the ultimately tragic ending.

THE MONOLOGUE:

Misha (sixteen) has been beaten by his father and caressed by the object of his affection, Lydia. While his father plugs himself in to the stereo in order to escape the sights and sounds of his home, Misha "confronts" him with his true feelings.

[Note: this monologue contains strong language]

TIME & PLACE:

Early 1970's. El Paso, Texas. The living room of the Flores family. Evening.

MISHA: Dad? . . . *Jefe*? *(no response)* For what it's worth, it wasn't just Mom who raised me. It was you, too, asshole. You're half to blame. You're the idiot who knocked her up, right? Your last name is mine, too, right? Everything about me you resent is half of you, too, motherfucker. So take some credit, Dad. I'm your son. I'm your decent well-raised second son. You bred me with fists and belts and shoes and whatever else you could throw at me. You raised me to jump at the sound of your voice and the stamp of your foot. You taught me to cower and shake and cover my ears in bed at night so I wouldn't hear Mom screaming while you slapped her. You taught me shame. I should grow up to be a spiteful little fucker just like you, hating the world for the crap I bring on myself, piling some real hurt on the people who care for me most. Except you know what, I won't. No sir, I won't be you. I don't know what the hell I'm gonna be and god knows I may turn out worse than I think, but I won't be you. Some day, not today, against my better sense, I'm gonna forgive you. You'll see.

LATINO
MONOLOGUE
1 M

THE PLAY:

The Soviet Union has collapsed, the "Iron Curtain" has come down and ideas like *perestroika* have begun to take root in the newly free societies. In Cuba, however, two sisters are released from prison only to remain under house arrest in their once-grand, now stark and utilitarian home. A piano remains the only reminder of their former lives—lives filled with music and literature and warmth and color, now turned to empty shells of memory and fast-fading hope. When the Lieutenant assigned to monitor the women arrives on the scene, the highly controlled lives of the three begin to swirl out of control—at least briefly—until, eventually, the cruel order is restored and the women are left with nothing.

THE SCENE:

Lieutenant Portuondo (thirties) is in charge of monitoring the Obispo sisters. He carries the letters that Maria Celia's husband writes in his bag, but he taunts her with their existence. He has struck a deal with her—if she "reads" him her next novel (the one she's not allowed to write so she simply carries it around in her head), he will give her a letter. One story/segment of the novel for one letter. It's a dangerous proposition, but she craves the news from her husband, so she agrees. His visits become more and more frequent and he becomes more and more friendly with the women as he lets down his guard.

TIME & PLACE:

Maria Celia and Sofia's house. The parlor. Evening. Cuba. 1991.

LIEUTENANT PORTUONDO: My old man . . . he left just like your father. Got fed up one day and said: "This isn't going anywhere." Got tired of waiting. He wanted to take me with him.

Yes. But I was already in the military.

Well sometimes I wonder what my life would've been like if I'd left. The poor man, ended up in some snowy town. Never married again after my mother died. He used to say he was old and didn't have any more heart left in him.—Was a good man, my father. Hard worker . . . Had an old Buick, used to travel the whole island selling milk containers to farmers. I used to help him on the road. Many a time, I saw his eyes water, when an old bolero used to play on the radio, and I'd ask him, "Why you crying, Pipo?" And he'd say, "I just saw Pucha, your mother, through the mirror." And I'd turn around to look and there'd be no one on the backseat. And he'd keep on telling me, "Oh, I know she's there, I can smell her sweet powder." It used to give me the creeps.

Knowing my father, he'd let go of the steering wheel and jump on the backseat with her.

You know, every time I come to this house I seem to forget the world. Something about you and your sister. You're different.

No, what I'm talking about is something in the blood.

Yes. What is it? What is that something that is passed on, that makes us who we are? I mean intelligence . . . grace . . . you're pure . . . You are who you are, unlike me. I don't know what I'm saying . . . ey, what would I know! I come from the middle of nowhere. A miserable town made of mud. Houses made of palm leaves. Dirt floor. No running water. I think people die there from looking at the cows. You know the only thing I liked about that place were the hurricanes. I loved the hurricanes. I was always waiting for the wind to blow hard enough and blow me away from there.

African Continent

The dialects of the continent of Africa are widely diverse. As different tribal groups were formed, migrated and then had their lands colonized by various other countries and people, their languages endured many changes and influences.

From *www.yellowpageskenya.com:* Over 30 distinct languages or dialects are spoken in Kenya. The main groups of tribes are the Bantu who migrated from western Africa, the Nilotic people who originated from Sudan and the Hamitic group, who were mainly pastoral tribes from Ethiopia and Somalia. The main tribes are Kikuyu (21%), Meru (5%), Kalenjin, Luyha, Luo (14%), Kisii, Kamba, Swahili, Masai, Turkana. The other large ethnic groups include the Luo, Luhya, Kamba and Kalenjin— There are also some groups of people who form a very small population. This includes the tribe of El Molo.

As seen, even within a single country in Africa, Kenya for example, the existence of at least three lingual groupings with many dialectal sub-groupings offers the listeners a variety of subtle nuances to the dialect of the region.

For our sound change chart purposes, we will be focusing primarily on the portions of Africa that were colonized by the British, so the learning of English would have occurred with a British flavor to the sounds. Though other influences can be heard in the dialects of some speakers, the "base" to which one should return is a British-English (not American-English) base.

Other regions in Africa were colonized by many different, primarily European, colonizers. When they came to Africa, they brought their original languages with them. It is not strange, therefore, to hear a Spanish-influenced, English speaking African dialect in one portion of the continent, and a Dutch-influenced, English speaking African dialect in another part. Indeed, as it has been noted that there may be over 1800 different languages in use on the continent of Africa, the dialect differences are just as vast and varied.

Perfect consistency in any dialect is difficult to find. Speakers who reside in the same dialect region will have individually unique speech patterns all to themselves. A Californian from San

Francisco, for instance, may sound completely different than a Californian from San Jose (45 miles south). The language is the same, the region is relatively the same, but there are other circumstances to take into consideration. The speaker's education, travel experience, family influences, occupation and social circles greatly influence the way the speaker will speak. The same is true for speakers of the African Continent dialect. This is not permission to be *unspecific* in your approach to and application of the dialect, but rather it is to encourage you to research the exact locale and language pattern of your character as defined in your script.

What follows are some sound changes that are heard when listening to some African speakers of English. Many changes are consistent throughout all speakers (such as "non-rhoticity"/ no "hard [r]" sound), and some changes are inconsistent even within the same speaker.

Thoughts on the African Continent Dialects

Sound/Music Thoughts

● There can be an alternative syllable stress pattern in multi-syllabic words. For example, words like "development" or "tropical" may become "deveLOPment" or "trohpiCAL."

● Multi-syllable stress can also occur in some words/places. For example, "particular" or "political" can become "pah tik yu lah" or "poh lih tee kahl," with each syllable pronounced with equal weight.

● Because of the lack of diphthongs in the two main vowel diphthongs ([oh] and [ay]), there can be a sense of quickness in the articulation of some syllables.

Mouth/Physical Thoughts

●To make the non-diphthong sounds [oh] and [ay], there can tend to be some tightening of the first part of the sound. Instead of allowing the mouth to lower and raise (they way those sounds are usually made in GAE), the jaw must remain in place and only the first part of the sound is spoken. See the "vowel changes" section for practice words.

● Because many of the dialects tend to be non-rhotic (the "r" sound is dropped at the ends of words and before consonants) the tongue can be relaxed behind the bottom teeth which will help with the release of throat tension.

Acting Thoughts

● Many selections from the African theatrical canon contain plays that require the combination of fantasy and reality . . . morality tales, animals who talk, and non-naturalistic

Kimberly Mohne Hill   199

circumstances can play heavily into the themes. It is important for the actor to be completely committed to the beauty of the storytelling and to allow for the childlike commitment to the imaginary worlds to be realized. Be unafraid to be physical, musical and mystical!

AFRICAN CONTINENT SOUND CHANGES

Remember, these sounds represent a listing of sounds that occur in many English-speakers on the Continent of Africa, but not all sounds occur in each speaker—you must choose the sounds appropriate for your character.

VOWEL CHANGES:

[ih] → *[ee]* *which, hills, rich* → *wheech, heels, reech*

[a] → *[eh]/[ah]* *fact, snack, bag* → *fect, snahk, bahg*

[ay] → *[e:]* *day, name, graze* → *de:, ne:m, gre:z*
(Lengthened and opened almost to an [a] sound. No diphthong.)

[uh] → *[ah]* *country, cup, from* → *cahntry, cahp, frahm*

[oh] → *[o:]* *go, rainbow, slow, hold* → *go:, re:n bo:, slo:, ho:ld*
(Lengthened and tightened. No diphthong.)

[u] → *[oo]* *look, woman, would* → *loook, woomahn, woood*
(Almost like sounding out the spelling of the word. It becomes a "long u" sound)

[ah/o] → *[oh]* *tropical, hot* → *trohpical, hoht*

VOWELS & DIPHTHONGS OF "R" CHANGES:

[er] → *[ah]* *her, stir, turmoil, nurse* → *hah, stah, tahmoil, nahse*
(Stressed syllable)

[er] → *[uh]* *mother, over, weather* → *mothuh, ovuh, weathuh*
(Unstressed syllable)

[ear] → *[ee uh]* *we're, steer, clear* → *wee uh, stee uh, clee uh*

[air] → [eh]   there, barefoot   →   theh, behfoot

[oor] → [oo uh] poor, endure   →   poouh, endyoouh

[ore] → [aw]   store, short, normal   →   staw, shawt, nawmal
(Very rounded)

[are] → [ah]   car, start, apart   →   cah, staht, apaht

CONSONANT CHANGES:

[th] → [d/z]   these, those, weather   →   dese, dose, weazuh

[th] →   [t/s]   things, path, nothing   →   tings, pas, noting

[z]   → [s]   please, bags, these   →   plees, begs, dese

[r]   sometimes trill red, around, great → rred, arround, grre:t

[ih] → [ee]
With the kids in the city, pick up his tickets. The trip to Windsor was windy.

[a] → [eh]/[ah]
Grab the man's bags and hand them to Cameron. Stand with the captain.

[ay] → [e:]
Stay at the play for the day. Major breakthroughs saved the lady.

[uh] → [ah]
From sun up to sun down, we run. The country was under his control.

[oh] → [o:]
Nobody knows how slow the road goes. It was so cold over in Rome.

[u] → [oo]
The good woman would have never stood there. Should we put the wood there?

[ah/o] → [oh]
We are not used to hot tropical stops. The cough was stopped by the doctor.

[er] → [ah]
The nurse had the worst service. The servant served her the first dessert.

[er] → [uh]
Mother and father were over each other. Together forever and ever.

[ear] → [ee uh]
Here dear, we're near the weird steer. The deer appeared fearful.

[air] → [eh]
The hare has a flare for decorating her lair. Stare at the chair by the stair.

[oor] → [oo uh]
I am sure, though poor, he will endure. The cure requires fewer lures.

[ore] → [aw]
The door of the store is on the floor. A retort from a short bore in court was reported.

[are] → [ah]
The car parked in the garden would not start. The scar on his arm is large.

[th] → [d/z]
The weather scared their mother. These are those that the others wanted.

[th] → [t/s]
The "Earth Theater" was ethical. The thirty thirsty things thought to say thanks.

[z] → [s]
Please put these bags with the king's. Those are hers and his are theirs.

[r] sometimes trill
Roll around the river and run over the ragged rocks. Read the red road map.

African Continent Dialect Audio References/Sound Samples

Internet Sources:

Internet sources can evolve and change over the years, so if any of the links below have expired, simply "Google search" the title of the link and you will be redirected to the updated site/location.

Ted Talks:

The Danger of a Single Story: http://www.ted.com/talks/lang/eng/chimamanda_adichie_the_danger_of_a_single_story.html

William Kamkwamba: How I built my family a windmill: http://www.youtube.com/watch?v=G8yKFVPOD6o

Joseph Lekuton: A parable for Kenya http://www.youtube.com/watch?v=qGIBN2gEIeU&feature=related

Ngozi Okonjo-Iweala: Let's have a deeper discussion on aid http://www.youtube.com/watch?v=bG2QKbpjDqo&feature=related

PBS Online:

www.pbs.org/frontlineworld/rough/2007/05/uganda_the_retu.html
www.pbs.org/frontlineworld/stories/uganda601
www.pbs.org/frontlineworld/stories/kenya

Speech Accent Archive: http://accent.gmu.edu/

IDEA Website: www.dialectarchive.com

CD's/Coaches:
Accents for Black Actors   Gillian Lane-Plescia
More Stage Dialects   Jerry Blunt

African Continent Monologues

Female

AFRICAN-CONTINENT
MONOLOGUE
1 F

THE PLAY:

Born to be a priestess, but forbidden to become one, Anowa marries the first man who asks her and then leaves her father and mother, vowing never to return. Her new, passive husband is surprised by his wife's strength, vision and opinionated carriage. When their fur-trading business begins to become successful, he decides to buy slaves to help him with his business—much to Anowa's horror and shame. As their wealth and her despair increases, she is haunted by the vision she had as a child—a vision that told her the only "children" she would ever bear would be the slaves that her husband bought. In the end, her ominous premonition becomes true—leading to a tragic conclusion for the husband and wife.

THE SCENE:

Anowa ("an aging young woman") remains dressed in the rags she wore when she first married her husband. She cannot bring herself to partake in the riches their business has created because her husband has purchased slaves to do all the work. Here, she reveals the vision she had as a child.

[Note: this monologue can be broken up into two smaller pieces if needed/desired]

TIME & PLACE:

Kofi Ako and Anowa's house. The central hall. Ghana, Africa. Day time.

ANOWA: *(as she speaks, she makes childish gestures, especially with her hands, to express all the ideas behind each sentence. She is talking to herself.)* I remember once. I think I was very young then. Quite young certainly. Perhaps I was eight, or ten. Perhaps I was twelve. My grandmother told me of her travels. She told of the great places she had been to and the wonderful things she had seen. Of the sea that is bigger than any river and boils without being hot. Of huge houses rising to touch the skies, houses whose foundations are wider than the biggest roads I had ever seen. They contained more rooms than were in all the homes I knew put together. Of these houses, I asked:

Tell me Nana, who built the houses?
She said:
Why do you want to know?
The pale men.
Who are the pale men?
I asked.
You ask too many questions.
They are the white men.
Who are the white men?
I asked.
A child like you should not ask questions.
They come from far away.
Far away from beyond the horizon.
Nana, what do they look like?
I asked.
Shut up child.
Not like you or me,
She said.
But what do they look like Nana?
I asked.
Shut up child or your mouth will twist up one day with questions.
Not like you or me?
Yes like you or me,
But different.
What do they look like, Nana?
What devil has entered into you, child?
As if you or I

were peeled of our skins,
Like a lobster that is boiled or roasted,
Like . . . like . . . but it is not good
That a child should ask questions.
Nana, why did they build the big houses?
I asked.
I must escape from you, child.
They say . . . they said they built the big houses to keep
the slaves.
What is a slave, Nana?
Shut up! It is not good that a child should ask big questions.
A slave is one who is bought and sold.
Where did the white men get the slaves?
I asked.
You frighten me, child.
You must be a witch, child.
They got them from the land.
Did the men of the land sell other men of the land, and
women and children to pale men from beyond the horizon
who looked like you or me peeled, like lobsters boiled or
roasted?
I do not know, child.
You are frightening me, child.
I was not there!
It is too long ago!
No one talks of these things anymore!
All good men and women try to forget;
They have forgotten!
What happened to those who were taken away?
Do people hear from them?
How are they?
Shut up child.
It is too late child.
Sleep well, child.
All good men and women try to forget;
They have forgotten!
    (pause)
That night, I woke up screaming hot; my body burning and
sweating from a horrible dream. I dreamt that I was a big,

big woman. And from my insides were huge holes out of which poured men, women and children. And the sea was boiling hot and steaming. And as it boiled, it threw out many, many giant lobsters, boiled lobsters, each of whom as it fell turned into a man or a woman, but keeping its lobster head and claws. And they rushed to where I sat and seized the men and women as they poured out of me, and they tore them apart, and dashed them to the ground and stamped upon them. And from their huge courtyards, the women ground my men and women and children on mountains of stone. But there was never a cry or a murmur; only a bursting, as of a ripe tomato or a swollen pod. And everything went on and on and on.

(pause)

I was very ill and did not recover for weeks. When I told my dream, the women of the house were very frightened. They cried and cried and told me not to mention the dream again. For some time, there was talk of apprenticing me to a priestess. I don't know what came of it. But since then, any time there is a mention of a slave, I see a woman who is me and a bursting of a ripe tomato or a swollen pod.

African-Continent
Monologue
1 F

The Play:

Set in South Africa in 2006, two women, one black (Beauty), and one white (Jennifer) meet in a farmhouse where Jennifer's beloved husband lay dying. Outside her window, a crowd has gathered to watch the government begin an excavation of her yard where the bones of tortured black citizens were buried over 35 years ago. As her husband lay dying, Jennifer is confronted with the truth that Beauty helps her to admit—her husband was one of the torturers.

The Monologue:

Beauty (twenties) begins to stir the memories inside Jennifer's mind as she reveals what she knows about the farmhouse and why the excavators are there.

Time & Place:

Present day. Johannesburg, South Africa. A farmhouse a little out of town. Late afternoon.

BEAUTY: *(to Jennifer [Mrs. Joubert])* Everybody is
very quiet
Mrs. Joubert
very . . .
upset. *(pause)*
Some people
are angry!
　　[Jennifer: Angry?]
Yes, angry *(pause)*
　　[Jennifer: Whose are they? The bones?]
Do you want me to say?
　　[Jennifer: Yes, if you know, yes.]
Jeffrey told us
years ago

this land
used to be
a farm.
    [Jennifer: A what?]
An old
farm.
Didn't
you know?
    *[Jennifer: No . . . I didn't know . . . I . . . I didn't
    know.]*
That p'raps
out on the edge
of the farm
there was
a bad place
an out house
an old cattle stall
quite big.
Police brought our people
here,
from the police station
many years ago
to question them
where their
screams
could not
be heard
to torture them
to kill them
Sometimes
they
burnt the flesh
then
buried the bones
in a pit behind
where the soil
was soft
and didn't
take much digging
Away from
prying eyes.

Kimberly Mohne Hill   211

AFRICAN-CONTINENT
MONOLOGUE
1 F

THE PLAY:

Set at a lamppost at a "crossroads," a host of artistic characters come and go as they examine the idea of the creative spirit and its blessings and curses. Can the Poet exist in the same world as the Cop? What is the role of the Painter? Why has society tried to silence the creative? What is the role of the Woman, the most "creative" of all? And what happens to the rest of us if they all cease to be?

THE MONOLOGUE:

Setting up the context and style of the piece, the first person to speak is The Woman (any age). The conceit of a "Prompter" who feeds her the lines as she maneuvers through the world of poetry and history and lyrical moments of dramatic confrontation is used so as to keep the narrative flowing. In this opening moment of the play, some of the poetry and passion is played out as the Woman attempts to find herself and make sense of her circumstances. She can tell the future, but is also cursed with remembering the past.

TIME & PLACE:

A lamppost. A crossroads. Anytime.

WOMAN: *(lying in a contorted position like an abandoned string puppet. Suddenly she lets out a cry)* What's happening to me? This is so odd. It feels like . . . No. And yet . . . This feels so strange. I have the impression I've already lived through this scene. One night. Exactly like this one. I stepped on this same stage. In these same lights. On this same set. And, I moved downstage as I'm doing now, and exactly like the other time, I . . . Yes, like the other time . . . I forgot my lines.

Yet it is the first time this has ever happened to me. Like so many things that happen only once but seem to have happened seven times over . . . When my friend Rachel died, I had lived through it all before. I relived it exactly as I am today. Like something starting over. That pain that hardens the throat like a lump of nausea, and the eyes like . . . like . . . No, it doesn't even hurt anymore, a pain like that doesn't even leave a wound. Not the slightest scratch on the belly. Not even a cramp. Not even a twinge. Not even . . . a wrinkle. It seems so stupid: you're innocently thumbing through the paper one day, and all of a sudden you come across "a young woman had her legs crushed in an automobile accident this morning at 10 a.m . . . ." And you refuse to recognize the young woman in the picture there in front of you. What the driver doesn't know is that a "young woman" is named Rachel, that she has a friend, that the evening of the accident someone might have made love to her and told her what beautiful legs she had. And that she is in love. What they don't know, all of those who are now telling her, "Thank God you're still alive" is that she is in fact dead. Because her life was dancing. Rachel is a friend of the best kind, the type you can say unpleasant things to when she happens by, just because you're in a lousy mood.

AFRICAN-CONTINENT
MONOLOGUE
1 F

THE PLAY:

Set at a lamppost at a "crossroads," a host of artistic characters come and go as they examine the idea of the creative spirit and its blessings and curses. Can the Poet exist in the same world as the Cop? What is the role of the Painter? Why has society tried to silence the creative? What is the role of the Woman, the most "creative" of all? And what happens to the rest of us if they all cease to be?

THE MONOLOGUE:

The Woman (any age) returns to wake us up, make us aware that even the Philosopher has fallen victim to silencing. What will happen to the world and it's people if we begin to lose all the essential elements of self-reflection and empathetic action?

TIME & PLACE:

A lamppost. A crossroads. Anytime.

WOMAN: Coming around a bend, I met a philosopher one day. He was standing there, haranguing an imaginary crowd. "Where were you when the books were waiting to be read? When the speeches filled with lies were waiting to be silenced? The crumbling building demanding beams and stones. It got words, words and good intentions, always the best of intentions. And sawdust and ashes. Perversion set in. One day man saw his ideal fall apart. He wasn't a man anymore. Searching, chasing, trying, rejecting, trying again. He got lost in the figures of his own calculations. Knowledge corrupted itself. It turned into indoctrination, blasphemy of the spirit. Where were you when the heroes who had vanquished the gods went to sit on the thrones, still warm. Here come our heroes. What are they saying? What are they predicting?"

Here comes the peddler with his bag of miracles. What is he selling? Ancestral masks, bits of colored glass turned dull and dusty, sunglasses for a sun that never appears. "Here comes the peddler. How much for these ancestral masks, for these clown masks? Ask for the latest invention, the surprise of the year, I named it the old age elixir and for the first hundred clients, a special gift, a trick mirror for luring birds. Get your tonic for premature aging, on sale at your authorized black market, at your local library and in children's bookstores, and in vending machines, get your old age tonic, your elixir of winter slumber, the balm that will close your eyes and turn them a deep pacific-paradise blue."

Scream. You want to scream. *(she opens her mouth in a scream but no sound emerges)* But you mustn't scream. Someone will hear your voice in the night and come gag you. What do you do not to scream? You turn on the television and a chill runs down your spine. It's time for the petrification-drug commercial. You open the paper; it's full of slogans for the eternal sleeping pill that will mummify you. On all the walls, there are giant posters for trick mirrors, new and improved.

Cry. You want to cry. *(She begins to cry but stops suddenly)* But you mustn't cry. What do you do not to cry? You laugh even if you don't feel like it. At all. *(She looks sad, then bursts out with a hysterical laugh. She stops abruptly)* But you mustn't laugh either. Someone will hear you and will somehow know that you can't fake anything, not even sleep.

RUINED

Lynn Nottage

AFRICAN-CONTINENT
MONOLOGUE
1 F

THE PLAY:

Set in a rain-forest bar/brothel in the Democratic Republic of Congo, Lynn Nottage's Pulitzer Prize Winning drama reveals the survival tactics of women in a world where men dominate in every way imaginable. Mama Nadi's bar provides respite and physical pleasures for the soldiers, rebels, politicians, and businessmen who come through—with no preference given to either "side" of the battle. It is dangerous and prosperous for Mama Nadi. For the women who serve as her "hostesses," she provides room, board and a community with a semblance of protection. They are all surviving as best they can in their cruel world.

THE MONOLOGUE:

Josephine (twenties) had been the "top girl" at Mama Nadi's until Sophie showed up. Because Sophie is "ruined" (soldiers captured and cruelly wounded her), she doesn't have to be with the men in the same way as the other women do. She only has to sing and look pretty. Mama Nadi will let no one touch her. Josephine lashes out at Sophie.

(Note: this monologue contains strong language/subject matter)

TIME & PLACE:

Living quarters behind the bar in a small mining town in the Democratic Republic of Congo. Present day. Morning.

JOSEPHINE: *(Josephine falls on the bed laughing)* Hey, *jo-lie fille.* (*Makes kissing sounds*) I can't talk to you? Who put you on the top shelf? You flutter about here as if God touched only you. What you seem to forget is that this is a whorehouse, cherie.

I'm sorry, but let me say what we all know, you are something worse than a whore. So many men have had you that you're worthless.
   (a moment)
Am I wrong? Am I wrong?
   (she confronts Sophie at the door)
My father was chief! My father was chief! The most important man in my village, and when the soldiers raided us, who was kind to me? Huh? Not his second wife: "There! She is the chief's daughter!" Or the crowds who pretended not to know me. And did any of them bring a blanket to cover me, did anyone move to help me? NO! So you see, you ain't special!

AFRICAN-CONTINENT
MONOLOGUE
1 F

THE PLAY:

Set in a rain-forest bar/brothel in the Democratic Republic of Congo, Lynn Nottage's Pulitzer Prize Winning drama reveals the survival tactics of women in a world where men dominate in every way imaginable. Mama Nadi's bar provides respite and physical pleasures for the soldiers, rebels, politicians, and businessmen who come through—with no preference given to either "side" of the battle. It is dangerous and prosperous for Mama Nadi. For the women who serve as her "hostesses," she provides room, board and a community with a semblance of protection. They are all surviving as best they can in their cruel world.

THE MONOLOGUE:

Salima (nineteen) has been working for Mama Nadi for over a month. Her husband, Fortune, has finally tracked her down and wants to take her back, rescue her, but she doesn't know it. Pregnant by the rebel soldiers who tied her to a tree in their camp and used her as a concubine for five months, she is afraid that when her husband sees her again, he will blame her, again. She recounts the day of her capture. (This monologue has been broken up into two parts because of length).

TIME & PLACE:

A month or so after starting to work at Mama Nadi's. Living quarters behind the bar in a small mining town in the Democratic Republic of Congo. Present day. Afternoon/early evening.

SALIMA: Do you know what I was doing on that morning? *(a calm washes over her)* I was working in our garden, picking the last of the sweet tomatoes. I put Beatrice down in the shade of a frangipani tree because my back was giving me some trouble. Forgiven? Where was Fortune? He was in town fetching a new iron pot. "Go," I said. "Go, today, man, or you won't have dinner tonight!" I had been after him for a new pot for a month. And finally on that day the damn man had to go and get it. A new pot. The sun was about to crest, but I had to put in another hour before it got too hot. It was such a clear and open sky. This splendid bird, a peacock, had come into the garden to taunt me, and was showing of its feathers. I stooped down and called to the bird: "Wssht, Wssht." And I felt a shadow cut across my back, and when I stood four men were there over me, smiling, wicked schoolboy smiles. "Yes?" I said. And the tall soldier slammed the butt of his gun into my cheek. Just like that. It was so quick, I didn't even know I'd fallen to the ground. Where did they come from? How could I not have heard them?

One of the soldiers held me down with his foot. He was so heavy, thick like an ox and his boot was cracked and weathered like it had been left out in the rain for weeks. His boot was pressing my chest and the cracks in the leather had the look of drying sorghum. His foot was so heavy, and it was all I could see as the others . . . "took" me. My baby was crying. She was a good baby. Beatrice never cried, but she was crying, screaming. "Shhhh," I said. "Shh." And right then . . . *(closes her eyes)* A soldier stomped on her head with his boot. And she was quiet.
(A moment . . . Salima release)
Where was everybody? WHERE WAS EVERYBODY?

Kimberly Mohne Hill   219

African-Continent
Monologue
1 F

The Play:

Set in a rain-forest bar/brothel in the Democratic Republic of Congo, Lynn Nottage's Pulitzer Prize Winning drama reveals the survival tactics of women in a world where men dominate in every way imaginable. Mama Nadi's bar provides respite and physical pleasures for the soldiers, rebels, politicians, and businessmen who come through—with no preference given to either "side" of the battle. It is dangerous and prosperous for Mama Nadi. For the women who serve as her "hostesses," she provides room, board and a community with a semblance of protection. They are all surviving as best they can in their cruel world.

The Monologue:

Salima (nineteen) has been working for Mama Nadi for over a month. Her husband, Fortune, has finally tracked her down and wants to take her back, rescue her, but she doesn't know it. Pregnant by the rebel soldiers who tied her to a tree in their camp and used her as a concubine for five months, she is afraid that when her husband sees her again, he will blame her, again. She recounts the day of her capture. (This monologue has been broken up into two parts because of length).

[Note: this monologue has strong language]

Time & Place:

A month or so after starting to work at Mama Nadi's. Living quarters behind the bar in a small mining town in the Democratic Republic of Congo. Present day. Afternoon/early evening.

SALIMA: I fought them! I did! But they still took me from my home. They took me through the bush - raiding thieves. Fucking demons! "She is for everyone, soup to be had before dinner," that is was someone said. They tied me to a tree by my foot, and the men came whenever they wanted soup. I make fires, I cook food, I listen to their stupid songs, I carry bullets, I clean wounds, I wash blood from their clothing, and, and, and . . . I lay there as they tore me to pieces, until I was raw . . . five months. Five months. Chained like a goat. These men fighting . . . fighting for our liberation. Still I close my eyes and I see such terrible things. Things I cannot stand to have in my head. How can men be this way?

   (a moment)
It was such a clear and open sky. So, so beautiful. How could I not hear them coming?

A peacock wandered into my garden, and the tomatoes were ripe beyond belief. Our fields of red sorghum were so perfect, it was going to be a fine season. Fortune thought so, too, and we could finally think about planning a trip on the ferry to visit his brother. Oh God please give me back that morning. "Forget the pot, Fortune. Stay . . ." "Stay," that's what I would tell him. What did I do, Sophie? I must have done something. How did I get in the middle of their fight?

AFRICAN-CONTINENT
MONOLOGUE
1 F

THE PLAY:

Using a controversial technique to help his patients deal with trauma, a psychiatrist encounters a special case in Azmera. Breaking the "doctor/patient confidentiality" by using her words to inspire changes in American-African foreign relations with all good intentions, Philip soon learns that changes do not occur quickly in bureaucracy, the media, or one's psyche . . . though "trancing" was supposed to have accomplished just that. In the end, it is Philip who is surprised that his own "genius" has been used against him . . . and that, ultimately, it was all for nothing.

THE MONOLOGUE:

Azmera (twenties) has come to Dr. Philip Malaad because he's "practically famous" for his techniques of therapy. In her second meeting with Dr. Malaad, she begins the memory work she has come here to confront as Dr. Malaad begins her "trance." (Note to actor: this is not a "hypnotic-zombie monotone" type of trance, it is more a state of extreme focus on the point, but with complete relaxation of extra stresses/tensions)

TIME & PLACE:

The present. A psychiatrist's office in Georgetown. Mid-Morning.

AZMERA: (*in a trance . . . to Philip*) . . . My pastor told us 'there are children living in sad little villages far away, and their parents aren't clever like ours. They drink rice liquor and quarrel at night instead of teaching the little ones to read, so if they rob us of our patience, we must ask Jesus to replenish our supply.'

[Philip: Was that helpful?]

I believe Jesus himself would have been tempted to give their hard little heads a smack. Any simple suggestion . . . like planting crops that stand up to the wind where the ground is more exposed . . . and they'd stare like you just advised them to stop growing rice and plant gingerbread cookies instead. They liked hearing stories from the Bible, although the idea that God could be everywhere at once struck them as stupid. Their gods are local. They'll pray to any ragged patch of weeds, if it grew along their river. That's why they'd rather nearly starve each winter than to move to where they'll be given two decent hectares of land. They like to wash in their own urine, can you imagine?

[Philip: It must have seemed like another world.]

They think a good soak toughens the skin, but it doesn't exactly make you want to snuggle up close to them at night.

African-Continent
Monologue
1 F

The Play:

Using a controversial technique to help his patients deal with trauma, a psychiatrist encounters a special case in Azmera. Breaking the "doctor/patient confidentiality" by using her words to inspire changes in American-African foreign relations with all good intentions, Philip soon learns that changes do not occur quickly in bureaucracy, the media, or one's psyche . . . though "trancing" was supposed to have accomplished just that. In the end, it is Philip who is surprised that his own "genius" has been used against him . . . and that, ultimately, it was all for nothing.

The Monologue:

Azmera (twenties) has returned to tell the real story of her church trip to Africa and how it fashioned her choices for the rest of her life . . . it's just not the story she had originally told the good doctor. She is still supposed to be "tranced" . . . but of course, she never was.

Time & Place:

The present. A psychiatrist's office in Georgetown. Late-afternoon.

AZMERA: I've been remembering things. Like that first summer in Kanta, with my church group . . . I was 17, just a child really, and I didn't want to go. I thought my friends will still be in London going to fabulous parties, and I'll have nothing to do at night. And that was true, but for some reason, when only three people in the group decided to stay an extra month, I was one of the three. *(slight beat)*
Then my first summer in graduate school, working on the Kanguya . . . I went with a few of the engineers to study a much older dam in the Congo. I asked out local guide what

he knew about the Jinti . . . animists who had been living there before the dam, and he pointed to the hills where trucks had taken them. We'd all seen aerial photos of dark, fertile soil on TV . . . so we knew the land in the hills was good. After work that day, the guide invited me to go out with him. I thought a restaurant and a bottle of wine, but he drove us to a ruined looking place that was full of shadows, and the shadows began to move. They were the Jinti who stayed behind. *(slight beat)*

They told me how officers made everyone dig up their own ancestors and pulverize the bones, before the trucks drove them into the hills. The hill land was a blistered tangle of scrub and rocks, but after awhile the women learned how to graze their buffalo and goats on the spiky grass, while the men scrambled all the way back down to the river . . . to keep farming the rich layers of silt along the banks, as they always had . . . as their *own* fathers . . . please . . . I'm almost done.

(slight beat)

Stories of how barren the hills were began reaching the capital, and soon the trucks were back. Men with shovels removed all the silt along the banks, then drove with it to the hills, so they could spread a thin layer over the ground . . . just thick enough to make it look like rich, black soil when the planes flew by to take pictures. So now there wasn't enough silt to farm along the river . . . and just enough in the hills to kill the grass that was keeping the goats alive. One by one the families left, hoping to find better land but ending up as squatters in abandoned buildings in forgotten towns.

(slight beat)

When the sun is out, the Jinti who are left move from shadow to shadow like ghosts . . . you can only tell they've gone by from a subtle change in the light. But that night they let me come near. Their faces had no definition . . . they were like inkblots, turning into the faces of the other Jinti they still remembered, the ones who were gone . . . then they turned again, and this time *I* remembered . . . faces from Kanta . . . faces I thought I'd forgotten, and then suddenly they began to fade, turning into ghosts . . . disappearing so slowly, it took me a moment to realize they were gone.

Kimberly Mohne Hill

AFRICAN-CONTINENT
MONOLOGUE
1 F

THE PLAY:

Set in the "Karoo Valley" in the Sneeuberg Mountains in South Africa, *Valley Song* is a love story of sorts—the love of a man for the land, a grandfather for his grand-daughter and a girl for her song. It is the story of old "Buks," a farmer, and Veronica, his granddaughter. She is his sole companion since his wife died. The songs she sings him bring him great joy and comfort in his old age, but they torment her as she feels caged in the valley, unable to leave to fully pursue her dreams. When her song is finally silenced by his refusing to let her go, Buks realizes that he must release her to her dreams in order to ever hear her song again.

THE MONOLOGUE:

Veronica (nineteen) wants to run away from the valley life that her "Oupa" (grandpa) seems perfectly content to live. She knows that she has a gift, her voice, and that her gift will wither and die if she is not allowed to leave and explore her options in a big city. When a buyer appears to be interested in buying the house and land that she and her grandfather farm, she is stunned to learn that her grandfather would want her to work as a servant in the house of the "master"!

TIME & PLACE:

Night. Outside the window of Sophie Jacobs where Veronica stands on an apple box to peep inside and watch the television. She talks directly to the audience.

VERONICA: *(to audience)* I hate those akkers. Yes. Hate them.

I know that's a big sin—to hate the Earth what God created —but I can't help it. That's the way I feel and that's what I want to say. If I was my Oupa I would rather let us go hungry than plant another seed in that ground. I mean it.

It gives us food, but it takes our lives. Oh yes it does! That's why my mother ran away. I just know it. She didn't want to live her life to be buried in that old house the way my Ouma's was. If ever anybody sees a spook in that house it will be my Ouma . . . scrubbing the floors. And my Oupa also—he'll spook those akkers one day. You'll see.

He's like a slave now to that little piece of land. That's all he lives for, and it's not even his. He talks about nothing else, worries about nothing else, prays for nothing else . . . "Come Veronica, let us hold hands and pray for rain." "Come Veronica, let us hold hands and pray that there is no late frost." "Come Veronica, let us hold hands and pray that bees don't sting the young pumpkins."

Well, what about me? I'm also a living thing you know. I also want to grow. What about "Come everybody, let us hold hands and pray that the bees don't sting the young Veronica."

Kimberly Mohne Hill   227

AFRICAN-CONTINENT
MONOLOGUE
1 F

THE PLAY:

Set in the "Karoo Valley" in the Sneeuberg Mountains in South Africa, *Valley Song* is a love story of sorts—the love of a man for the land, a grandfather for his grand-daughter and a girl for her song. It is the story of old "Buks," a farmer, and Veronica, his granddaughter. She is his sole companion since his wife died. The songs she sings him bring him great joy and comfort in his old age, but they torment her as she feels caged in the valley, unable to leave to fully pursue her dreams. When her song is finally silenced by his refusing to let her go, Buks realizes that he must release her to her dreams in order to ever hear her song again.

THE MONOLOGUE:

Veronica (nineteen) has saved almost half of the train fare into Johannesburg. She tells her grandfather of her plan to leave, and he is not receptive in the way that she had hoped.

TIME & PLACE:

Buks and Veronica's home. Night. The present.

VERONICA: *(to her grandpa/"Oupa")* No. I earned it. I sing my songs for them and they pay me. *(Misinterpreting Buks' silence and thinking she can bring him over to her side)* It's true. They all like my singing. They say I got a good voice and that I must go somewhere where there is a singing teacher so that I can take lessons and make it better. That's why I wrote to Priscilla. And you heard what she said in her letter Oupa . . . there's plenty of jobs in Johannesburg so I'll be able to get work and pay for my singing lessons —because if I become a very good singer Oupa I can make lots of money. People who sing on the TV and the radio get paid a lot of money. Just think Oupa! You can even come up there as well then if you want to . . . forget about those old Landman akkers and come and live in Johannesburg in a proper house with a big garden . . .

> *(she takes a chance, fetching the tin with her savings, opening it and placing it trustingly on the table in front of her Oupa)*

Look Oupa—I nearly got half the price of a train ticket already.

I'm doing it because I want Oupa to be proud of me. I want to give you something back for all you've given me. But I can't do that if I stay here. There's nothing for me in this Valley. Please try to understand what it is like for me. I'll die if I got to live my whole life here.

AFRICAN-CONTINENT
MONOLOGUE
1 F

THE PLAY:

Set in New South Africa (post-apartheid), the play follows the story of two young, disposed friends—Vicky and Freddie— as they embark on a night of drunken thievery. When they seek to rob Vicky's mother's former employer, Lionel, they are caught and in defense, they hold him captive. As the evening progresses, Freddie's desire to be a "Master" like Lionel is played out in a frighteningly ominous charade—with Vicky acting as Freddie's "girl," serving him his meal and calling him "Master."When Lionel is shot and killed, accidentally, the play ends with Freddie leaving Vicky alone singing gospel hymns and crying for her mommie.

THE SCENE:

Vicky (sixteen) responds to Lionel's pleas for her to remember how she had possibilities once, a better future once.

TIME & PLACE:

The dining room of a comfortable house in a small Karoo village. Late night. The present.

VICKY *(to Lionel)*: It's not easy Lionel. Maybe if I had all your big words I could maybe tell you. But . . . (*she shakes her head*). [I can speak to him] Because he already knows. When I speak to Freddie I'm just talking about things he already knows in his heart. That is where it is Lionel. In our hearts. Your heart lives here in this nice big house. Freddie's heart and my heart live all our lives in matchboxes in Pienaarsig. There's no hope for us there, Lionel. When *you* wake up in the morning you look out of your big window you see your flowers and the fruit trees and you feel happy. When we wake up in the morning and look out of our dirty little windows we see hungry dogs and another day with no hope. When we go to sleep at night . . . nothing has changed. There's no place for hope in a matchbox, Lionel. And because we got no hope . . . We don't care. We don't care about nothing no more, Lionel.

No. Don't shake your head, Lionel like we are saying something bad. Because I can see what you think in your eyes, Lionel. Ja. All those times we were talking about me going back to school, learning typewriting and all the other things, I could see in your eyes that you also had no hope for me. I wasn't the only one telling lies, you were also. Those times when I asked you for money when there was no food in the house because Pa had spent all his money again on getting drunk . . . but I could see you didn't believe me.

Hope?

African Continent Monologues

Male

AFRICAN-CONTINENT
MONOLOGUE
1 M

THE PLAY:

Born to be a priestess, but forbidden to become one, Anowa marries the first man who asks her and then leaves her father and mother, vowing never to return. Her new, passive husband is surprised by his wife's strength, vision and opinionated carriage. When their fur-trading business begins to become successful, he decides to buy slaves to help him with his business—much to Anowa's horror and shame. As their wealth and her despair increases, she is haunted by the vision she had as a child—a vision that told her the only "children" she would ever bear would be the slaves that her husband bought. In the end, her ominous premonition becomes true—leading to a tragic conclusion for the husband and wife.

THE SCENE:

Kofi Ako (a young man) has made a strong business from the use of slaves. His wife, Anowa, is violently opposed to the purchase of people and she will not relent in her criticism of him. As his anger mounts, he controls his urge to hit her.

TIME & PLACE:

Kofi Ako and Anowa's house. Ghana, Africa. Day time.

KOFI AKO: *(letting go of Anowa)* Hmm. How sad . . . And yet if I gave you two good blows on your cheeks which flashed lightning across your face, all this foolishness would go out of your head. *(to himself)* And what is wrong with me? Any man married to her would have by now beaten her to a pulp, a dough. But I can never lay hands on her . . . I cannot even think of marrying another woman. O it is difficult to think through anything. All these strange words!

Anowa, what is the difference? How is it you can't feel like everybody else does? What is the meaning of this strangeness? Who were you in the spirit world? *(laughing mirthlessly)* I used to like you very much. I wish I could rid you of what ails you, so I could give you peace. And give myself some.

It is an illness, Anowa. An illness that turns to bile all the good things of here-under-the-sun. Shamelessly, you rake up the dirt of life. You bare our wounds. You are too fond of looking for the common pain and the general wrong.

Anowa, you are among women my one and only treasure. Beside you, all others look pale and shadowless. I have neither the desire nor wish to marry any other, though we all know I can afford dozens more. But please, bring your mind home. Have joy in our overflowing wealth. Enhance this beauty nature gave you with the best craftsmanship in cloth and stone. Be happy with that which countless women would give their lives to enjoy for a day. Be happy in being my wife and maybe we shall have our own children. Be my glorious wife, Anowa, and the contented mother of my children.

AFRICAN-CONTINENT
MONOLOGUE
1 M

THE PLAY:

Set in South Africa in 2006, two women, one black (Beauty), and one white (Jennifer), meet in a farmhouse where Jennifer's beloved husband lay dying. Outside her window, a crowd has gathered to watch the government begin an excavation of her yard where the bones of tortured black citizens were buried over 35 years ago. As her husband lay dying, Jennifer is confronted with the truth that Beauty helps her to admit—her husband was one of the torturers.

THE MONOLOGUE:

A Boy (seventeen) opens the play as he answers questions posed to him by the unseen interrogators. We don't know his fate until the end of the play.

TIME & PLACE:

1969. Johannesburg, South Africa. Night.

[A slash (/) indicates where the lines had been broken up in the original text. Slashes are used to save page space in this reprinting, they are not necessarily acting or vocal notes]

(A young black boy—his hands are tied behind his back . . . he is being interrogated)

BOY: I don't know/twenty maybe/twenty at first/Yes/didn't I just/tell you/Baas?
Water,/about the water/mainly,/other things of course,/but a child/had died/drinking/
from the tap/they thought/so/they called/a meeting/The leaders/The leaders/
of the Residents Association/*(more agitated)*/You know/ who they are,/everyone knows./
It's no secret/who they are/Of course I know her,/I am/her son/I am/her son/No!/I don't know
that person/No/I don't know/his name/I . . . /I have/never/ met him!/All the people/Yes/the residents/
they . . . /Spilled/Yes, they spilled out,/onto the football pitch/Twenty at the meeting/but outside/
there were . . . /others/Just others/other people/At first,/they were all/young men/I don't know/
maybe/a hundred/Of course/I remember exactly/what they were doing/They were singing/
and dancing/that's all/ small boys/climbed/onto their brother's backs/bouncing/up and down/
in fun/And one/old man,/thin as sticks,/rode his grandson/ like a mule,/banging tins/like drums,/
baring his gums/and laughing—/And so/they clapped/all of them/and danced/And some of them/
they sang/Baas/*(terrified)* Why am I here?/Why/have you brought me/here?/to this / terrible/ terrible/place? *(for the first time his eyes acknowledge two other men present)*/I told you/ everything, mybasé/ at the police station/ *(he looks up)* What/ are you doing?/ Truly,/
I have nothing/ to tell you/ Truly.

AFRICAN-CONTINENT
MONOLOGUE
1 M

THE PLAY:

Set at a lamppost at a "crossroads," a host of artistic characters come and go as they examine the idea of the creative spirit and its blessings and curses. Can the Poet exist in the same world as the Cop? What is the role of the Painter? Why has society tried to silence the creative? What is the role of the Woman, the most "creative" of all? And what happens to the rest of us if they all cease to be?

THE MONOLOGUE:

The Poet (any age) tells us about his friend, the Painter, and the way his art was silenced . . . much the way the Poet feels his art is being silenced, too.

TIME & PLACE:

A lamppost. A crossroads. Anytime.

POET: Suspect. Suspect. There's that word again. As far back as I can remember, it's the same old story. Nostrils flaring like a bulldog smelling bad meat. Suspect. Like my friend the painter. He was classified suspect too. Because he used to draw pictures that people didn't always understand. So the cops would raid his place from time to time. They would tear up his books and notes and slash his paintings. Since they never found anything there, they started searching inside him, cutting him up into little pieces. We'd see the painter after that, busy gluing himself back together, remolding, replastering his body. I was a child. I watched. He said it was to intimidate him they'd done that. I asked him, "Sir, what does intimidate mean?" One day he came back and discovered that among the pieces he'd gathered and started gluing together, he couldn't find his tongue. And that was it. He'll never say another word. Not a single word. He can only smile. He's the one who taught me how to smile and even to laugh, laugh about anything, about myself, my mistakes, my misfortunes. He taught me how to smile. He said that only real smiles count. A smile doesn't lie. You can't smile cynically or cruelly. That's just like a grimace, nothing more. You roll up your lips like you roll up your sleeves to start beating somebody. No one is fooled. He taught me to see too. He had eyes made to see. The enormous eyes of a poet, big as oceans. And full of things. And cloudy. When they looked at you, you felt transparent. He taught me to see through opaque and closed surfaces, to turn things inside out. They didn't like his eyes here. They found them suspect. They said his eyes were gadgets for spying, hidden cameras, witch's eyes, the eyes of a clairvoyant, of a voyeur. So it goes. He smiled because he didn't realize they would tear his eyes out . . . *(he collapses)*

AFRICAN-CONTINENT
MONOLOGUE
1 M

THE PLAY:

Set at a lamppost at a "crossroads," a host of artistic characters come and go as they examine the idea of the creative spirit and its blessings and curses. Can the Poet exist in the same world as the Cop? What is the role of the Painter? Why has society tried to silence the creative? What is the role of the Woman, the most "creative" of all? And what happens to the rest of us if they all cease to be?

THE MONOLOGUE:

Finally, the Prompter (any age) reveals to us that he is actually, quite possibly, the voice of the Playwright. The scenes just played before us were meant to stir us into passionate defense of the art and study of the Humanities. Did it work, or does he have to play it out for us again? Here he struggles with his effectiveness in sending out his message.

TIME & PLACE:

A lamppost. A crossroads. Anytime.

PROMPTER: Enough. Enough. Twenty years this has been going on, twenty years of starting over, again and again. Every evening the same play runs through my mind, the same image of actors putting on the mask, the costume, the emotions of characters. Characters. But this isn't about characters. It's about me. I am the Poet. This story playing in my mind is my history.

Twenty years in the dark, in this prison where everything disappears. Where only memory remains. Repetitive, crazed, careless memory that I keep goading, prompting, whispering it words and pictures to save them from forgetfulness.

Henceforth I am only memory. That's been my only means of existence ever since I was given a box of matches and a script written in my own hand. A double turn of the key and everything is settled for eternity. My words, my words . . . my gestures were convulsive but my words . . . I believed in them a long time ago, in their power to reduce pain to its essence, to a strict minimum . . . and to compensate for absence with illusion.

Memory. Yes, memory is needed for all the vanishing species of mankind. The poet . . . disappeared. The traveler . . . disappeared. The painter . . . disappeared. The philosophers . . . disappeared. The priest . . . disappeared. Who's next? But there's no one left. Who's turn?

This evening I'd like to stop it all there. Rid my mind of these obsessive memories. Stop everything. Escape. Leave before it's too late, before you, the last surviving species, disappear. Get out. I know the ending, it's always the same. The end, the end, the end . . .

THE HERD

Charlotte-Arrisoa Rafenomanjato

AFRICAN-CONTINENT
MONOLOGUE
1 M

THE PLAY:

Drought has taken over Faly's village. When his suggestion for bringing drinking water back to the village is met with
violent opposition (the Chief's sons are exploiting the drought
for personal gain), he runs away to the City. His attempts to
blend in with this new "herd" prove to be more difficult than
he imagined. Though it seems backwards to Faly—the City
gives away water for free and sells things like cakes and places
to sleep—Faly finds himself being questioned by police when
he attempts to help carry loads to earn some money. In the end,
he is released to return home to his village.

THE MONOLOGUE:

Faly (twenty-six) has decided to seek his fortune in the City.
His first night is met with some astonishment as he learns the
difference between City hospitality and village hospitality. He
slept on the street. His attempt to earn money are misunderstood
as robbery and he is taken to the police station. Here, he tries to
explain the truth of what happened.

TIME & PLACE:

A police station in the city. Afternoon. Africa. Anytime. Far
(two day's walk) from Faly's tribal village.

[Police Inspector: (violently) Be quiet! . . . You'll answer me when I ask you something! . . . (to Faly) So you left your village to continue your thievery in the city?)]

FALY: No, Sir. Rango's daughter had died of thirst; Rasoa's children didn't have anything to eat just so they could have a drop of water . . . so, I thought it was a good idea to suggest requisitioning the wagons . . . but Ravo, Doda, and Haga started fighting . . . The Chief became very angry and wanted to call the police . . . I was frightened and ran away. In town, I followed two men who'd offered me a place to stay; they stole everything I had. I wanted to see you, Sir Police, but there were too many cars, I was afraid to cross the street . . . I was hungry; Raozy offered me some cakes. I wanted to find some work, but there are no herds in the city. *(he stops and looks around him in every direction)*

[Police Inspector: (kindly) Go on, I'm listening.]

I wanted to help a man carry his suitcases to earn a bit of money. He left them right near me and ran off . . . two men beat me up . . . I was locked up in a dark room with some very big men, it was stifling . . . there wasn't any sun, it was dark all the time . . . I am no thief, Sir Police, I don't want to go back in that black pen with that herd of shadows . . . My father told that the rain has returned and that we have spades and plows. It's the sowing season, there's much work to do in my village, please, I beg you . . . let me go home. Blanche must be waiting for me.

[Police Inspector: Who is Blanche?]

She's the only white cow in the herd, just as I'm the only dwarf in the village. But she was smarter than me, she stayed right with the herd . . . and if she hadn't what would have become of her?

LES BLANCS

Lorraine Hansberry (adapted by Robert Nemiroff)

AFRICAN-CONTINENT
MONOLOGUE
1 M

THE PLAY:

White missionaries have settled in a nameless African community. Their presence, while helpful to some, has grown to be oppressive to others. Education, medicine, and religious instruction have bent the culture of the community to one of a more "European" feel—much to the growing resentment of some of the local tribesmen. When the leader of the Resistance dies, his sons come home to bury him and they discover that they have grown apart in more ways than one. While one found his calling in the cloth of the religious order who raised him, the other found his purpose in the distance between his European life and his African roots. A third brother, with a secret heritage of his own, seems to be the only brother willing to fight against the "invaders." The call to take up their father's arms in the cause of the resistance is met with confusion, disillusion, despair and ultimately, resolve . . . resulting in the eventually tragic end of the brothers relationship.

THE SCENE:

Tshembe Matoseh (twenties) has returned from Europe for his father's burial. Here, he talks with the white reporter from America who is at the Mission to do a story about the Mission's leader.

TIME & PLACE:

A Mission Compound somewhere in an African country which exists "solely in the imagination of the author." Sometime after "curfew" (8:30 p.m.). "The time is yesterday, today tomorrow—but not very long after that."

TSHEMBE: *(casting his eyes up with a sigh of utter resignation)* Oh dear God, why? Why do you all *need* it so?! This absolute *lo-o-onging* for my hatred! *(a sad smile plays across his lips)* I shall be honest with you, Mr. Morris. I do not "hate" all white men—but I desperately wish that I did. It would make everything infinitely easier! But I am afraid that, among other things, I have *seen* the slums of Liverpool and Dublin and the caves above Naples. I have *seen* Dachau and Anne Frank's attic in Amsterdam. I have seen too many raw-knuckled Frenchmen coming out of the Metro at dawn and too many pop-eyed Italian children—to believe that those who raided Africa for three centuries ever "loved" the white race either. I would like to be simple-minded for you, but—*(Turning these eyes that have "seen" up to the Other with a smile.)*—I cannot. I have—*(touches his brow)*—seen. *(Suddenly, wearily closing his eyes)* Mr. Morris, mostly I am tired. I came home for sentimental reasons. I should not have come. *(A beat. Smiling with his own thoughts)* My wife is European, Mr. Morris . . . a marvelous girl. We have a son now. I've named him Abioseh after my father and John after hers. And all this time I have, mainly, been thinking of them. In the future when you tell some tale or other of me will you take the trouble to recall that as I stood here, spent and aware of what will probably happen to me, most of all I longed to be in a dim little flat off Langley Square, watching the telly with my family . . .

> [Charlie: Then all this talk about freedom and Africa
> is just that . . . talk!
> Tshembe: Isn't that what you wanted, Mr. Morris, to
> talk? Charlie: Yes but I thought . . .]

You thought! You thought because I am a black man with a black skin that I have answers that are deep and pure. *(dismissal)* I do *not!*

AFRICAN-CONTINENT
MONOLOGUE
1 M

THE PLAY:

A folkloric look at ambition and loyalty: a man seeks to provide enough meat for his entire village for months, but on his hunt, instead of finding food, he finds a tortoise which appears to sing. Thinking he will make his fortune and win the respect and admiration of his wife and the king, he brings the tortoise home, only to find it won't sing for anyone else. His manipulative father-in-law hears a voice singing and attributes it to the tortoise, which he then claims as his own. His ambitions are thwarted, however, by the fool who brings it to the King's attention that his chief councilor is thinking about becoming King himself. When the tortoise refuses to sing for anyone, and the father-in-law goes to jail, the Fool reveals that the singing tortoise was actually the man's own voice warning him about getting over-ambitious. The King orders everyone to "listen to your tortoise."

THE MONOLOGUE:

Agbo-Kpanzo (any age) has gone into the forest to hunt for a feast for his village and his wife. Three days and three nights later, he is empty-handed. He curses the spirits who have brought him so low.

TIME & PLACE:

An unreal forest. Any time. After three days and three nights of hunting and near-starvation.

[An unreal forest. Agbo-Kpanzo, alone, speaks in an incanta-
tory tone, with emphatic gestures to the invisible spirits who
fight against him]

AGBO-KPANZO: You know me, all of you! I'm Agbo-Kpanzo!
Agbo-Kpanzo! Hey, hey, hey, Agbo-Kpanzo! Agbo-Kpanzo
never misses the mark. Agbo-Kpanzo never comes back
empty-handed. Agbo-Kpanzo's not afraid of lions. Lions
are afraid of Agbo-Kpanzo. Agbo-Kpanzo's not afraid of
buffalo. Buffalo are afraid of Agbo-Kpanzo. Agbo-Kpanzo,
hey, hey, hey, Agbo-Kpanzo! Spirit of the Forest, Spirits of
the Winds, of the Rivers, of the Streams, and you, who are
the soul power of the lion, the buffalo, the elephant. I know
who's stirred you up against me. I know it's in the name of
my enemy that you're playing these dirty tricks on me. For
three days and three nights, I've been wandering through
the forest without finding any game worthy of my prowess.
And after I'd promised the village I'd bring back choice
meat! I'd provide them a month of feasting! My enemy
knows this. He knows, too, that if I keep my promise, the
whole village will sing my praises, and the King, perhaps,
will appoint me to the much sought after position of Chief
Councilor. So my enemy, who's my own father-in-law, has
unleashed all the powers of the occult to bring about my
humiliating failure, to make me come back empty-handed
so the villagers, instead of with praise songs, will greet
me with ridicule: "Today the crocodile couldn't satisfy his
stomach with even a shrimp." They'll go so far as to forget
the mountains of meat I've brought them before. That's the
way of the world.

But you've miscalculated, you demon spirits and you, my
enemy, my dear father-in-law, who've called them up.
Agbo-Kpanzo's going to win. I'm Agbo-Kpanzo, He-Who-
Fears-Neither-The-Lion-Nor-The-Buffalo-Nor-The-Elep-
hant! Even if I have to stay in this forest a week, a month,
three months, I'm going to win.
(a pause . . . something moves just a few steps away
from him)

Kimberly Mohne Hill 247

Ah, now I've got you! Don't move! You're a goner!

(Whatever it is, moves)

A tortoise? All you are is a tortoise? A funny-looking tortoise? Are you really a tortoise, or are you someone disguised as a tortoise? Speak up! Lord help me, you look like a real tortoise! For starters, I'm going to kill you.

American Southern

When we talk about an American Southern dialect, we are most likely referring to the sounds of the people who are native to that region of the United States which exists south of the "Mason-Dixon Line." The states often included in the geographic delineation of "Southern States" are: Alabama, Arkansas, Georgia, Kentucky, Louisiana, Mississippi, North Carolina, Oklahoma, South Carolina, Tennessee, Texas, Virginia, and West Virginia. The northern part of Florida can also be considered "Southern" for the purposes of dialect study, but as a whole, this state is a unique area of sound and speech collections due to the large number of retirees from other states choosing to live out their years in the mild climate of Florida.

With the advancement of the internet and the spread of "instant access" technology, the voices and speech patterns of many different people are readily available at any given moment in time. Due in part to the strength of the film and television industry in America (and with it, a "general American/Californian" sound in the speech patterns of many actors), and the advancement of the technology sector in many southern metropolitan communities, the old, thicker southern accents are beginning to soften and adapt to a more non-region specific sound. In places like Austin, Texas or Atlanta, Georgia, for example, the younger generations of speakers may have a broader, more "general" American accent as opposed to the syrupy southern drawl that we most closely identify with a "Southern accent."

It is important to acknowledge that when some people attempt a "Southern accent," they occasionally shift into a stereotypical sound. The reason the sound becomes a stereotype is because the actor is *judging* the character and the region. For example, when asked, many people will associate a British accent with a person who is "intelligent or superior"—these are *judgments* not based on truth about the *individual*, but based on broad stereotypes of a long line of people. The same judgment occurs when people are asked about a Southern accent—judgments may include "not educated, racist, crude," etc. It is this judgment that prevents the speaker from fully embracing the personal truth of the dialect sounds of the character. The choices and sounds become *caricature*, not a *character*. Be careful to avoid these judgments!

American actors, at some point of time in their careers, will have to do a Southern accent. It is practically unavoidable. So many great plays have been written both *about* the South and *by* Southern authors that one would have to consciously attempt to avoid them in order to go without ever doing a Southern dialect! Characters in the plays that you will be performing, however, range in *time period* from contemporary southern to classic southern. It will be up to you, the actor, and your director to discern which accent your character is to speak. As with each dialect you study, you must read the entire play and character descriptions in order to accurately place your accent. What follow are some general sound substitutions that should give you a wide representation of the sounds of the South!

MOUTH/ PHYSICAL THOUGHTS

● Southern "soft r" dialects are done with relaxation in the lips and tongue. This will give you a feeling of total facial/throat relaxation. This does not equal a lack of energy, but rather an ease in the speech and rhythm of the dialect/character. This dialect can feel relaxing and comfortable.

● Southern "hard r" dialects contain more tongue tension and, therefore, some jaw tension can result. Be sure to warm up and relax your jaw muscles thoroughly before diving into a "hard r" dialect.

SOUND/MUSIC THOUGHTS

● The Southern Drawl is achieved by saying a slight "uh" sound before or after you say a vowel sound (like the sound "ee" may become "ee$_{uh}$"). It is not separate from the pure vowel, but is done almost at the same time as the vowel . . . very quickly and subtly. The vowel sound "moves around" a bit.

● Depending on where you are, the pace of the Southern dialect can vary from all the extremes: incredibly quick and piercing to slow and "syrupy." There are many different paces of speech which lie in the middle of those two extremes.

ACTING THOUGHTS

● If you overdo the drawl or the relaxation element of the dialect, your character will seem stereotypical and caricature. Be careful.

● Remember, Southerners are proud, eclectic, warm, compassionate, strong, and spirited—there is no "one" type of Southerner. They are all *individuals* with individual histories. They just happen to live in one of the most history—rich areas of the United States and, therefore, share that common story to some degree.

Kimberly Mohne Hill

- Subtlety works very well in this dialect. You may not need to change much in your own speech pattern to achieve this dialect. In fact, adopting only a few of the suggested changes may give you enough of a "Southern" sound to lend your character some credibility.

AMERICAN SOUTHERN DIALECT SOUND CHANGES

SOUTHERN VOWEL CHANGES:

ih	→	ee_{uh}	give, wind	→ g ee_{uhv}, w ee_{uh}nd
eh	→	ih	ten, men	→ tin, min
a	→	a /ayuh (drawled)	man, planned	→ ma yuhn, pla yuhnd
uh	→	uh	(relaxed) stuck, love	→ stuhk, luhv
oo	→	$_{uh}oo$	routes, news	→ r $_{uh}oo$ ts, n $_{uh}oo$ z
oh	→	$_{uh}oh$	goes, show	→ g $_{uh}oh$ z, sh $_{uh}oh$
aw	→	ah	awesome, all, broad	→ ahsome, ahl, brahd
ah	→	aw oo (drawled)	gone, dog	→ gaw oon, daw oog
eye	→	ah	night, fly, find	→ naht, flah, fahnd
ay	→	$_{uh}ay$	late, day, grain	→ l $_{uh}ay$ t, d $_{uh}ay$, gr $_{uh}ayn$
ow	→	a	how, now, found	→ ha, na, fand

THE QUESTION OF "R"

Vowel of [r] is dropped in some regions (usually east of the Mississippi River), hardened in others (especially Oklahoma and Texas)

ear	→	eer (or) eeuh	here, dear	→ heer, deer (or) heeyuh, deeyuh
air	→	ayer (or) ayuh	there, fair	→ thayer, fayer (or) thayuh, fayuh
or	→	ohr (or) owuh	your, more	→ yohr, mohr (or) yowuh, mowuh
are	→	are (or) ah	cart, farther	→ cart, farther (or) caht, fahthuh
er	→	er (or) uh		→ werd/wuhd, over/ovuh, sir/suh

OTHER CHANGES:

[ing]	→	[in]	biking, hiking, farming	→ bahkin', hahkin', farmin'

[ih] → [ee$_{uh}$]:
Phil pinned Jim and hit 'm. My kin lives 'n the middle of Dixon near Gimlet.

[eh] → [ih]:
The men entered the tent and then went to bed. The pen is empty again.

[a] → [a / a yuh]:
Stand by your man, ma'am. The family camp in the Hampshires is fancy.

[uh] → [uh (relaxed)]:
I got stuck in the mud in my truck. It's fun to chew gum in the sunshine.

[oo] → [$_{uh}$oo]:
Who're you to be so rude to the crew? Ooops! The cartoon fool just flew in the pool.

[oh] → [$_{uh}$oh]:
My beau, Bo, knows a whole lot. No, I don't know where to go. I don't eat oats.

[aw] → [ah]:
The audition was awful when the author talked. I saw Dawn talking to Paul.

[ah] → [aw oo]
Doggone it! The monster is long gone. The song about the donkey was on a lot.

[eye] → [ah]:
My mind flies when I spy the night sky. Try to find the right five pines up high.

[ay] → [$_{uh}$ay]:
The game is charades. I made paper angels for the table. Take the cake to Amy.

[ow] → [a]:
Around town, I wear a crown. How now brown cow? Wow! A mountain house!

[ear] → [eer / ee_{uh}]:
Steer clear of weird types of beer, ya hear? We cheered when they cut his beard.

[air] → [ayer /ayuh]:
They're not aware that the bear is there. Careful there! Tear the stairs down.

[or] → [ohr or ohuh]:
I adore him, so I ignore the snore. The storm forced the corps to swarm toward home.

[are] → [are or ah]:
Start carting the parts to the hardware store. Darts harm large art and farmers.

American Southern Dialect Audio References/ Sound Samples

INTERNET SOURCES:
Internet sources can evolve and change over the years, so if any of the links below have expired, simply "google search" the title of the link and you will be redirected to the updated site/location.

International Dialects of English Archive—www.dialectsarchive.com

Library of Congress—American Memory—"After the Day of Infamy"—http://memory.loc.gov/ammem/afcphhtml/afcphseries.html

Library of Congress- American Memory—"Voices from the Days of Slavery"—http://memory.loc.gov/ammem/collections/voices/vfssp.html

Library of Congress—American Memory—"American English Dialect Recordings"—http://memory.loc.gov/ammem/collections/linguistics/title.html

American Folklife Collection—http://www.loc.gov/folklife/onlinecollections.html

Veteran's History Project—http://www.loc.gov/vets/stories/

University of Southern Mississippi Oral History Project—Freedom" http://www.youtube.com/user/USMOralHistory

University of Southern Mississippi Oral History Project—Surviving Katrina" http://www.youtube.com/user/USMOralHistory#p/u/4EfKtvHB-_kQ

Southern Foodways Oral History Project—(Click on a "star," click on "read the oral history," and then scroll to the bottom for a link to the sound sample attached to the history) http://www.southernfoodways.com/documentary/maps/index.html

FILM/TV SOURCES:Southern Film List—http://en.wikipedia.org/wiki/List_of_films_set_in_the_Southern_United_States

FILMS:
(for a more extensive list, divided by region, see Ginny Kopf's book, *The Dialect Handbook*)

True Grit	*The Blind Side*
The Princess and the Frog	*We Are Marshall*

The Notebook *No Country for Old Men*
The Secret Life of Bees *Glory Road*
Forrest Gump *Monster's Ball*
Steel Magnolias *Man in the Moon*
Double Jeopardy *The Color Purple*
Midnight in the Garden of Good and Evil
The Divine Secret of the Ya-Ya Sisterhood

TV:

Friday Night Lights
The Golden Girls
Designing Women

American Southern Monologues

Female

AMERICAN SOUTHERN
MONOLOGUE
1 F

THE PLAY:

The first of a trilogy, *August Snow* introduces us to the lives and loves of the Avery family from eastern North Carolina. It's 1937 and Neal Avery just married his sweetheart, Taw. The newlywed period is ending, though, after only one year. Taw's insistence that her husband give up his youthful ways seems to push him further away from her. His mother doesn't help, instead, she blames Taw for her son's restlessness and hopes that he will return home. In the end, he decides to try to put his childishness aside and regain his wife's trust and esteem. How long it will last remains to be seen.

THE MONOLOGUE:

Taw (twenty-one) just gave Neal an ultimatum: "choose your friend Porter and your youthful ways, or choose me." If he chooses Porter, she will leave him tonight. He has the day to think about it. She presents her reasoning to us.

TIME & PLACE:

The kitchen of the one-room apartment that Neal and Taw rent. 6 a.m. Neal has been out all night and has just come home, somewhat still intoxicated. Taw asked him to leave and to choose between her or his friend. Eastern North Carolina. August, 1937.

TAW: Since I was an orphan so early in my life, I taught myself to avoid most dreams—dreams at night, good or bad. They seemed one strain I could spare myself; and I honestly think, in all these years, I've never had two dozen dreams—not to speak of. Neal dreams like a dog by the stove when he's here, the rare nights I get to guard his sleep. Last night though when I finally dozed, sad as I was, I lived through a dream as real as day.

I'd finished my teacher's diploma and was ready to save the world around me, all children. What thrilled me was *that*— they were all young and not too hard yet to help. I'd show them the main thing an orphan knows—how to tuck your jaw and brave hails of pain and come out strong as a good drayhorse or a rock-ribbed house on a cliff by water.

But once I entered my class the first day and trimmed my pencil and faced the desks, I saw they'd given me twenty grown men—all with straight sets of teeth. I prayed I was wrong, that I'd got the wrong room. Still I said my name, and the oldest man at the back of the room stood tall at last in a black serge suit and said "Don't wait another minute to start. We've paid our way."

I had a quick chill of fright that I'd fail; but then I thought of the week they died—my mother and father, of Spanish flu—and I knew I did have a big truth to tell, the main one to know.

I opened my mouth and taught those grown men every last fact an orphan needs and learns from the day she's left— courage and trust and a craving for time. They listened too but hard as I looked in all the rows, I never saw Neal.

IN THE RED AND BROWN WATER

Tarell Alvin McCraney

AMERICAN SOUTHERN
MONOLOGUE
1 F

THE PLAY:

The first in the trilogy of Brother/Sister plays, *In the Red and Brown Water* introduces us to a community in San Pere, Louisiana. This first story is primarily centered on Oya, a young woman with a bright future in the sport of track and field. When a "man from state" comes to offer her the chance to attend his school on a scholarship, she must regretfully decline due to her mother's illness. After her mother dies, it is too late to attend the school as they have already given the scholarship to the next girl on the list. With no college, no mother, and no one to help her maneuver the tricky waters of young adulthood, she falls prey to the local "ladies man," Shango. After he abandons her, she marries the safe man, Ogun Size. The pang of childlessness, the desire for the man who left her and the slow realization that she is stuck in the life she's living serve to drive her insane.

THE MONOLOGUE:

The "Man from State" has just offered her a scholarship at his school so she can run track for them, but Oya (late teens) must decline.

Acting Note: This play is written in such a way as the actors speak their stage directions. When speaking the stage directions, the actors should do it in character. There is no delineation/ parenthetical markings to tell you where the stage directions are, you must simply be aware of the change in delivery/context.

TIME & PLACE:

The distant present. La Pere, Louisiana. Oya's home.

OYA: Oya looks out forward. Head high.
        I don't know how to say this sir. Yes I
        Do. First I say thank you, sir, very much I
        Wish I could come on with you this year I do.
        I love to run. Nobody loving kicking
        Up dirt on a track like me. That I know,
        That I feel. But I love my mama. And
        She been low lately. Low. She say she ain't
        Got long. I don't believe her but I do.
        And sir you don't know but I'd be lying
        If I say I wouldn't go crazy if something
        Happened to Moja while I was away.
        She say just a year, this year. I stay
        With her this while. I will that's what I will do.
        But I'll keep training keeping running, always
        Running. I know there might not be a chance
        Next year but there might be. But there may not be
        Moja when I got back . . . So I'ma stay here. To
        See her stay or . . . go. Thank you so much sir.
        Have a good year.

IN THE RED AND BROWN WATER

Tarell Alvin McCraney

AMERICAN SOUTHERN
MONOLOGUE
1 F

THE PLAY:

The first in the trilogy of Brother/Sister plays, *In the Red and Brown Water* introduces us to a community in San Pere, Louisiana. This first story is primarily centered on Oya, a young woman with a bright future in the sport of track and field. When a "man from state" comes to offer her the chance to attend his school on a scholarship, she must regretfully decline due to her mother's illness. After her mother dies, it is too late to attend the school as they have already given the scholarship to the next girl on the list. With no college, no mother, and no one to help her maneuver the tricky waters of young adulthood, she falls prey to the local "ladies man," Shango. After he abandons her, she marries the safe man, Ogun Size. The pang of childlessness, the desire for the man who left her and the slow realization that she is stuck in the life she's living serve to drive her insane.

THE MONOLOGUE:

When Lil' Legba gets an older woman pregnant, he asks Oya (now twenties) if it's right to be bringing babies into this world. This is her response.

(Note: this monologue contains strong language)

Acting Note: This play is written in such a way as the actors speak their stage directions. When speaking the stage directions, the actors should do it in character. There is no delineation/ parenthetical markings to tell you where the stage directions are, you must simply be aware of the change in delivery/context.

TIME & PLACE:

The distant present. La Pere, Louisiana. Oya's home.

OYA: What else we got to do? Nothing. Sit around
       Watch the world. Babies got some sunshine in em.
       I saw some little bowlegged baby
       Walk round here the other day just as cute
       I looked at her and I said, "Whose baby is this? . . ."
       She looked at me, "Not yours . . . " She wasn't mean
       She just say it matter of fact and bent down
       Picked one of them firecrackers left from the Fourth
       I say, "Lil baby don't eat that."
       She put it right in her mouth and started chewing
       Like it was this brand-new flavor Now and Later
       Just chewing and the burnt orange of the gunpowder
       Flowing out her mouth . . . she just smiling.
       Her mama walk by and grab up the baby,
       "What the fuck you got in your mouth?"
       Starting spanking her.
       "Didn't I tell you to not put shit in your mouth . . ."
       The baby start crying. She carrying the baby away look-
       ing at
       Me talking bout, "And you just gon sit here and let her kill
       herself?"
       I wanted to be like, "Bitch that ain't my baby
       She just told me I wasn't her mama . . ."
       Why she let the baby just roam around the projects
       Any damn way? As much as they shoot round here?
       Letting your child just walking around here. Unchecked!

Kimberly Mohne Hill   265

Insurrection: Holding History

Robert O'Hara

American Southern
Monologue
1 F

THE PLAY:

Ron's great-great-grandfather is a miraculous 189 years old. When his family gathers for his birthday party, his great-great-grandson seems distracted, wrestling with the demands of his life at Columbia. When Ron goes to say goodbye to his "gramps"—a man who has been silent for over 75 years—he hears the old man ask him to "take me home." Thus begins a physical (and metaphysical) journey for Ron and his gramps, TJ, back in time to the days of Nat Turner and southern slavery. Ron gets to live and witness "first-hand" the story his great-great-grandfather lived as young man. He begins to see, through the events of the time leading up to Nat Turner's Revolt, that he is not simply writing a paper for a class about slavery, but he is writing "his-story."

THE MONOLOGUE:

Ron's cousin, Octavia (eighteen) has endured the snide innuendoes about her possibly being pregnant all night. Now, she lets her mama know what is really growing inside her.

TIME & PLACE:

Somewhere in Virginia. Present-day. Night time. After the birthday party.

OCTAVIA: let me say this one last time
   i ain't nowhere near pregnant

   I have somethin' inside of me tryin' ta git out and it ain't
   no baby!

   you just cain't bring yo' mind to dreamin' that I might do
   somethin' with myself beside layin' around havin' babies
   stayin' in this backwoods town

   i gats plans!!!
   whether you believe it or not i'm goin' ta college
   i'm gon' make somethin' of myself I'm gon git out of
   this town
   just lak ronnie

   (Oscar-winning) . . . this ain't slavery times mama.
   I ain't some slave gul on some farm that cain't move
   'less somebody tell her she can move
   cain't no man take me less I want 'im ta
   and I don't haveta pick nobody's cotton
   I'm free
   ya ga that?
   my mind is free
   you heah that? mama
   my. mind
   is. free
   ain't that what that commercial say?
   i can be ALL i can be?
   I can do whateva I set my mind ta do
   I'm not limited
   by the people 'round me

Alfred Uhry

AMERICAN SOUTHERN
MONOLOGUE
1 F

THE PLAY:

The play begins in Atlanta on the eve of the star-studded opening night of the movie, *Gone with the Wind*. It is December 1939, and Hitler is just beginning his rise in Germany. For the family of Adolph Freitag, the holidays bring more of a concern about who will take his nieces to the traditional Ballyhoo Dance. His niece, Lala, lives in a fantasy world of *Gone with the Wind* obsessions and a severe inferiority complex—she may never get anyone to take her to the dance. Sunny, the "favorite" of her uncle Adolph, comes home for the holidays from college and before she even arrives at home, she has a date to the dance! Themes of internal favoritism, class-ism and ultimately the perspective of what truly matters in life are handled with grace and depth by each of the characters in this story.

THE MONOLOGUE:

Sunny (twenties) has always looked "less Jewish" than her cousin, Lala—at least, that's what Lala tells her. When her uncle's new employee, Joe, comes down to Atlanta from New York, he sees her family's Christmas Tree in the living room, presents underneath, and he questions her commitment to her faith. She, tired of being accused of trying to hide her origins, responds with a story from her youth.

TIME & PLACE:

The living room of her family home in Atlanta. December, 1939. There is a Christmas tree in the room. Everyone else has gone upstairs to bed. It's about 11:30 pm.

SUNNY: The summer between sixth and seventh grade my best friend was Vennie Alice Sizemore. And one day she took me swimming at the Venetian Club pool. Her parents were members. So we were with a whole bunch of kids from our class and the boys were splashing us and we were all shrieking—you know—and pretending we hated it, when this man in a shirt and tie came over and squatted down by the side of the pool and he said, 'Which one is Sunny Freitag?' and I said I was, and he said I had to get out of the water. And Vennie Alice asked him why and he said Jews weren't allowed to swim in the Venetian pool. And all the kids got very quiet and none of them would look at me.

I got out of the pool and phoned daddy at his office. When he came to get me all the color was drained out of his lips. I remember that.

[Joe: And Vennie Alice?]

Oh, her mother called up Mama and apologized. We stayed friends—sort of. Neither of us ever mentioned it again, but it was always there. So believe me, I know I can't hide being Jewish.

Liars, Thieves, and other Sinners on the Bench

Jo Carson

American Southern
Monologue
1 F

The Play:

A collection of vignettes and characters from her site-specific, theatrical, documentary-style performance pieces, *Liars, Thieves . . .* is a collection of some of the most haunting voices and stories that Jo Carson was able to witness. Though based on real conversations, Jo uses theatricality and creativity to depict the very real worlds she observed. These stories allow the actors to simply speak and simply believe. In the simplicity, there is beautiful and meaningful resonance.

The Monologue:

A woman (any age) recalls how a childhood accident paved the way for a childhood obsession. [*Note to the actors: It is up to you to do the imagination work on these pieces with regard to the details of the place, the people you are speaking to, and the past that led you up to this moment in time. With no narrative to guide you, the limit is your imagination.*]

Time & Place:

Newport News, Viriginia. The present.

A WOMAN: I may have been six, and I had been warned not to play with matches, that they were not toys and that I could hurt myself with them. But I watched my mother put a box of matches away in the pantry, and I climbed up on a chair after her and got a handful of them. I took them out between the house and the barn and I struck them, all of them at once, they made a huge flame in my hand and I got very frightened and I pulled my hand into my side. I put the flame out with that gesture, but I made a burn on my side, the scar is still there.

My father found me, crying, evidence of what I had done at my feet, the burn in my dress and my side. He didn't get mad, but he explained that what I had done was very dangerous, that fire could go everywhere, especially if there was something like kerosene to help spread it. We had kerosene in the barn, I knew we did.

Everywhere. I thought about our house. We could go to the barn if the house caught fire, except if the fire went everywhere, the barn was part of everywhere.

We could go to our neighbor's house. But that was part of everywhere.

We could go to the church, to the school, but that too was part of everywhere.

I lay in bed that night, my side still hurt with the burn, and tried to think of somewhere that wasn't part of everywhere.

That night and many, many more nights, long after the burn had healed.

It was the problem of my childhood. It became my obsession, to think of the somewhere that wasn't part of the everywhere a fire could go.

Somewhere safe.

In the way of children, I did think of a place. I had been to Maryland once to visit my grandfather, and we could go to his house. It was far enough away that maybe it wasn't a part of the everywhere my father spoke about, it was in another state and surely fire couldn't go there . . . If fire came, we would go to Maryland.

But I knew better, I could tell myself Granddaddy's house was safe during the day, but in my dreams at night, fire came to Maryland, too . . . .

Jo Carson

American Southern
Monologue
1 F

The Play:

A collection of vignettes and characters from her site-specific, theatrical, documentary-style performance pieces, *Liars, Thieves . . .* is a collection of some of the most haunting voices and stories that Jo Carson was able to witness. Though based on real conversations, Jo uses theatricality and creativity to depict the very real worlds she observed. These stories allow the actors to simply speak and simply believe. In the simplicity, there is beautiful and meaningful resonance.

The Monologue:

A preacher's wife (any age) confesses her sinful reaction to the generosity of her husband's flock. [*Note to the actors: It is up to you to do the imagination work on these pieces with regard to the details of the place, the people you are speaking to, and the past that led you up to this moment in time. With no narrative to guide you, the limit is your imagination.*]

Time & Place:

Colquitt, Georgia. The present.

THE PREACHER'S WIFE: Most of the time, after a sermon, Jack would be invited to dinner somewhere with one of the congregation, and you never knew what you were going to get to eat because people in the church took turns feeding the preacher, and some of them didn't have so much as others, and some of them looked at feeding the preacher as an obligation to be got through and not as something to be given joyously. I didn't go with him much, I had my children to tend to, and children would have been an extra burden on the family that was feeding him.
Some of these churches were so poor that people never paid a preacher in money, they'd give him what they call a "pantry shower" and he'd take his pay home in food.

Well, this once, the children were at his mother's, and I went with him to Sunday dinner. We got to the house, and as we were going in, the woman picked up a previously used cud of tobacco off the front porch rail and put it in her mouth. And we got inside, and there was a sort of sand pile around the woodstove, and that was where she spit. There was an old red dog that came in with us and he laid down in the sand pile, in the spit—it was warm, you know—and he rolled over a lot to scratch his back, got up and shook, and laid back down again.

That was hard for me.

And she started putting stuff on the woodstove to warm it. It was all cooked already, it just wanted warming. And that dog, well . . . I saw she had some sweet potatoes, and I figured I could eat one of them because they still had the skin on them and I could peel it off and eat the inside, but it turned out they weren't for Sunday dinner, they weren't cooked yet, they were for supper and what was for dinner was chicken and dumplings in what looked like dishwater. She served up the chicken and dumplings in bowls.

I didn't dare look at the bowls or the spoons.

Remember, all the time she has this tobacco in her mouth and she's spitting. And the dog is rolling and shaking. And I know I can't eat this. I can't do it. And the truth is, I don't want Jack to eat it either, but I can't stop him, and he sees it as his duty to partake of what is offered. And I know I'm going to lie to get out of it, and I just hope the Lord doesn't get too mad at me. This is a sort of love offering but maybe it is better to refuse it than it is to throw it up.

So I took a fainting spell. I'd seen them but I'd never had one, and if I say so myself, I took a good one. I had to go outside for air. And then I just couldn't eat a thing, couldn't even drink a glass of milk. I sat in a chair away from the table for dinner while they ate. Jack did his duty and claimed it wasn't as bad as it looked.

Then, going home, he said he knew I faked a fainting spell, and I told him it was the dog that did it.

And he said I was raised picky.

And I said I was raised clean, and didn't intend to change.

And he said most of life is not as clean as you seem to think it ought to be, and you're going to have to get used to it if you eat dinner with me at these country churches.

And I said fine. Fine, fine, fine. And I have not gone with him to another of those Sunday dinners yet.

Kimberly Mohne Hill   273

SEE ROCK CITY

Arlene Hutton

AMERICAN SOUTHERN
MONOLOGUE
1 F

THE PLAY:

A sequel to *The Last Train to Nibroc,* here we get to see the continued journey of the young couple—May and Raleigh—as they start their married life. The war has come to the front steps of May's family home when her younger brother re-enlists for a second tour after being sent home with an injury from his first tour. Surely, they wouldn't send him to Normandy . . . Meanwhile, Raleigh's writing career faces rejection after rejection and May loses her esteemed position as school principal to the men returning from the war. As they endure the stresses and strains of a young married couple and the pressures of the outside world, their relationship shows its strength when May, selflessly, encourages Raleigh to leave their small town and go to live in New York in order to start his writing career off in a real way.

THE MONOLOGUE:

May (twenties) attended a meeting where her future was revealed to her. With the war over, she would need to find a new meaning/purpose for her life. Her old job would be going to the returning veterans.

TIME & PLACE:

Mid-May, 1945. Evening on the front porch of May's parents' home in Corbin, Kentucky. With her husband, Raleigh.

MAY: All they do is trade war stories. It was. It was useless. It was the most useless meeting ever. It's . . . I don't know . . . They're gonna . . . it's a . . . a . . . structure, they called it. I'm gonna . . . And Margaret Shirley's not retiring until after another school year. Another whole year. They talk about the war for about a half an hour. Finally they stop. The superintendent's just sitting there looking at me. We're gonna adjust the structuring, he said. What's that, I ask. I think he's talking about building a new building or something. That's what I asked, what kind of structure? Well, they said, reassignments. Paint Lick's going to have a new principal. A new principal. The high school and the element'ry. I must have been sitting there with my mouth just, just hanging open, I was so shocked. Last meeting they told me, the superintendent told me, what a good job I was doing and all. So I'm thinking, oh, they must be transferring me. And the thoughts are just flying through my head—what are you and I going to do, will we have to move, will it be more money. And then the . . . And the superintendent says to me, well, the war's almost over, and the boys are coming home so you can go be a housewife now, as if that were something I should really want to do. *(straight to Raleigh)* I didn't mean it that way. I didn't mean—

I said what do you mean? I still didn't get it. And they looked at each other and sort of nodded, all fake-sympathetic. I have good news, he said. You won't have to work so hard, anymore. I told him I don't mind working hard. *(straight to Raleigh)* I don't. I do. I work very hard. Wasn't about that. He said again, the war's over. And I said, I know the war's over and that means there'll be more boys at school now. But I can handle them. Don't worry about that. And they laughed and one of them, a fat ole guy said, I'm sure you can, little lady. And I still didn't get what they were telling me. The war's over. What's that mean? We're all happy about that. I was thinking all this as I was just staring at them. As if they'd asked me some question I couldn't answer. And they said, well, the superintendent said, our boys are back now, and they need jobs.

Yes. David Johnson's going to be the new principal at the school. What school will I be at, I asked. You'll be . . . they look at a piece of paper as if they didn't know already. You'll be replacing, if you want to, Margaret Shirley. She'll be retiring. Teaches second grade. Second grade. And not for another year, even. She's retiring, but not for at least another year, maybe two.

Then they said, if you want to come back. Want to come back, I asked. Where am I going? They smiled and said with a year off you'll probably be starting a family, won't you. That's my business, I said. No, we have to make it our business, they said. We're giving all the principal and assistant principal jobs to returning soldiers. The ones old enough to have been in college are officers and they'll make good principals and we have to support our boys who fought for us. And I was just trying not to cry.

Kimberly Mohne Hill   275

Stories I Ain't Told Nobody Yet

Jo Carson

American Southern
Monologue
1 F

The Play:

A collection of vignettes and characters from her site-specific, theatrical, documentary-style performance pieces, *stories I ain't told nobody yet* is a collection of some of the most haunting voices and stories that Jo Carson was able to witness. Though based on real conversations, Jo uses theatricality and creativity to depict the very real worlds she observed. These stories allow the actors to simply speak and simply believe. In the simplicity, there is beautiful and meaningful resonance.

The Monologue:

Female (any age) remembers her mother's role in the family.

[Note to the actors: It is up to you to do the imagination work on these pieces with regard to the details of the place, the people you are speaking to, and the past that led you up to this moment in time. With no narrative to guide you, the limit is your imagination.]

Time & Place:

Present day. East Tennessee.

6: It was a Saturday and my mother was cooking.
    She always cooked on Saturday
    for us and for her bachelor brother
    who came by on Sunday afternoon
    and got his casseroles for the week.
    None of them used tuna fish, mushrooms, peas . . .
    there was a list of things he wouldn't eat.
    We were not allowed to be so picky.

    By Sunday they'd be frozen.
    All he had to do was keep them frozen
    and put them in the oven one at a time.
    His were labeled, he knew what he was going to eat.
    For herself, she looked into the frozen layers
    and tried to remember.
    I don't know why she did it.
    He was perfectly capable of doing
    anything else he set his mind to.
    He could have learned to cook.

    This Saturday
    she was up to her elbows again in family and food.
    I heard her in the kitchen. "No," she said.
    After a moment: "I'm honored, but no thanks."
    Another moment: "No, thank you, no, no, no."
    I asked who she was talking to. She said,
    "I'm practicing my speech for the circle,
    they are planning to ask me to be president."

    I thought she was very silly practicing
    her public speaking with a series of emphatic no's
    as she stacked casseroles in her freezer.
    "No!" to the macaroni and cheese and tomatoes.
    "No!" to the broccoli and concentrated celery soup
    "No. No. No."

    It was twenty years before I understood
    she was trying to learn how to say it.

Kimberly Mohne Hill   277

STORIES I AIN'T TOLD NOBODY YET

Jo Carson

AMERICAN SOUTHERN
MONOLOGUE
1 F

THE PLAY:

A collection of vignettes and characters from her site-specific, theatrical, documentary-style performance pieces, *stories I ain't told nobody yet* is a collection of some of the most haunting voices and stories that Jo Carson was able to witness. Though based on real conversations, Jo uses theatricality and creativity to depict the very real worlds she observed. These stories allow the actors to simply speak and simply believe. In the simplicity, there is beautiful and meaningful resonance.

THE MONOLOGUE:

Female (any age) uses the lessons from her life to warn the "next woman."[Note: This monologue contains strong language]

[*Note to the actors: It is up to you to do the imagination work on these pieces with regard to the details of the place, the people you are speaking to, and the past that led you up to this moment in time. With no narrative to guide you, the limit is your imagination.*]

TIME & PLACE:

Present day. Appalachia/East Tennessee.

29: I cannot remember all the times he hit me. I might could count the black eyes, how many times I said I ran into doors or fell down or stepped into the path of any flying object except his fist. Once I got a black eye playing softball. The rest were him. Seven, eight. I can name what of me he broke: my nose, my arm, and four ribs in the course of six years' marriage. The ribs were after I said divorce and in spite of a peace bond. I spent the night in the hospital. He did not even spend a night in jail. The sheriff I helped elect does not apply the law to family business. He always swore he never meant to do it. I do believe he never planned. It was always just the day, the way I looked at him afraid. Maybe the first time he did not mean to do it, maybe the broken ribs were for good luck.

I want to post this in ladies' rooms, write it on the tags of women's underwear, write it on coupons to go in Tampax packages, because my ex-husband will want to marry again and there is no tattoo where he can't see it to tell the next woman who might fall in love with him. After six months, maybe a year, he will start with a slap you can brush off. Leave when he slaps you.

When he begins to call you cunt and whore and threatens to kill you if you try to go it will almost be like teasing but it is not. Keep two sets of car keys for yourself. Take your children with you when you go. If he is throwing things, he is drinking. If he is drunk enough he cannot catch you. A punch in the breast hurts worse than a punch in the jaw. A hit with an object does more damage than a hit with a fist unless he is so drunk he picks up a broom instead of a poker. If you pick up the poker, he will hit you with it. He probably will not kill you because you will pass out, and then, he is all the sudden sorry and he stops. When he says he will not hit you again as he drives you to the hospital, both of you in tears and you in pain, you have stayed much too long already. Tell the people at the hospital the truth no matter how much you think you love him. Do not say you fell down stairs no matter how much he swears he loves you. He does love you, he loves you hurt and he will hit you again.

AMERICAN SOUTHERN MONOLOGUES

MALE

AUGUST SNOW

Reynolds Price

AMERICAN SOUTHERN
MONOLOGUE
1 M

THE PLAY:

The first of a trilogy, *August Snow* introduces us to the lives and loves of the Avery family from eastern North Carolina. It's 1937 and Neal Avery just married his sweetheart, Taw. The newlywed period is ending, though, after only one year. Taw's insistence that her husband give up his youthful ways seems to push him further away from her. His mother doesn't help, instead, she blames Taw for her son's restlessness and hopes that he will return home. In the end, he decides to try to put his childishness aside and regain his wife's trust and esteem. How long it will last remains to be seen.

THE MONOLOGUE:

Neal (twenty-two) has to decide between his best friend and his wife. His wife will leave him if he chooses his best friend, and his best friend has just confessed that he will wait for him forever. Neal ponders the state of his life and the attraction other people have for him.

TIME & PLACE:

The Downtown Café. 1:30 pm. A small town in Eastern North Carolina. August, 1937.

NEAL: One thing I know I'm not is conceited. So believe what I say, in this one respect. The trouble, my whole life, has been this—people fall for me, what they *think* is me. They mostly call it love, and it generally seems to give them fits. They think life can't go on without me—when I know life can go on in the dark if they blind you, butcher you down to a torso, stake you flat on a rank wet floor and leave you lonesome as the last good soul.

Neal Avery can't save the *shrubbery* from pain, much less human beings. It may be the reason I act so bad to Taw and my mother and Porter, my friend. It may be why I'm soaked to the ears so much of the time—*I know I'm me*, an average white boy with all his teeth, not Woodrow Wilson or Baby Jesus or Dr. Pasteur curing rabies with shots.

Who on God's round Earth do they think I am? Who would patch their hearts up and ease their pain? If I stand still here for many years more, won't they wear me away like the Sphinx or a doorsill, just with the looks from their famished eyes?

If I wasn't a Methodist, if this wasn't home, wouldn't I be well advised to strip and run for the nearest desert cave and live among wolves or crows or doves? Wouldn't they simply elect me gamekeeper?

Am I ruined past help? Could I take ten steps on my own—here to there—much less flee for life, for my good and theirs?

AMERICAN SOUTHERN
MONOLOGUE
1 M

THE PLAY:

The first of a trilogy, *August Snow* introduces us to the lives and loves of the Avery family from eastern North Carolina. It's 1937 and Neal Avery just married his sweetheart, Taw. The newlywed period is ending, though, after only one year. Taw's insistence that her husband give up his youthful ways seems to push him further away from her. His mother doesn't help, instead, she blames Taw for her son's restlessness and hopes that he will return home. In the end, he decides to try to put his childishness aside and regain his wife's trust and esteem. How long it will last remains to be seen.

THE SCENE:

Worried that her husband may choose to stay with his old ways and continue partying and hanging out with his best friend, Porter (twenty-two), Taw goes to enlist Porter's help in convincing Neal to return to her and work on their marriage. After Taw leaves, Porter reveals his motivations for sticking with his friend.

TIME & PLACE:

4:30 pm. After Taw leaves. The back alley behind Avery's Clothing store—where Neal and Porter work. A small town in Eastern North Carolina. August, 1937.

PORTER: In a town this size, everybody's known your family since the Seven Years' War; so you have to live most of your life in code—little signs and fables for the kind and wise, not actual touch or plain true words. That's been all right by me most times; it keeps you from having to make up your mind too fast, or ever.

For years you can walk around some strong magnet and never ask why or be told to explain. Then when you least expect it, somebody you've known from the dark of the womb will step up and reach for the trunk of your life and shake it like a cyclone, and you'll shed your apples in full public view.

It happened to me my first year in high school, fourteen years old-English class, of course. Miss Speed Brickhouse went round the room asking everybody what they hoped to be; and everybody answered in some sensible way—storekeeper, bank teller, practical nurse. Then she called on me—"Porter, what's your plan?"

I was already helping at Avery's Store—Neal and I on Saturdays—and I figured I'd sell men's clothing for life. But what I said was what slipped out. To Miss Speed's withered face, and twenty-six children vicious as bats, I said "I hope to be a lighthouse for others."

Miss Speed tried to save the day by saying the church was the noblest career, but everybody knew she was wrong, and they *howled*—right on through Commencement three whole years later.

I found the strength to hold my ground though, and I never explained. I knew I'd found, and told, the truth—a real light, for safety, in cold and high seas.

Not for *others* though; I lied in that—just for Neal Avery, the one I'd long since chosen as being in special need and worthy of care. I may well have failed.

Kimberly Mohne Hill

IN THE RED AND BROWN WATER

Tarell Alvin McCraney

AMERICAN SOUTHERN
MONOLOGUE
1 M

THE PLAY:

The first in the trilogy of Brother/Sister plays, *In the Red and Brown Water* introduces us to a community in San Pere, Louisiana. This first story is primarily centered on Oya, a young woman with a bright future in the sport of track and field. When a "man from state" comes to offer her the chance to attend his school on a scholarship, she must regretfully decline due to her mother's illness. After her mother dies, it is too late to attend the school as they have already given the scholarship to the next girl on the list. With no college, no mother, and no one to help her maneuver the tricky waters of young adulthood, she falls prey to the local "ladies man," Shango. After he abandons her, she marries the safe man, Ogun Size. The pang of childlessness, the desire for the man who left her and the slow realization that she is stuck in the life she's living serve to drive her insane.

THE MONOLOGUE:

Ogun Size (twenties) is a nice, solid, hard-working young man who truly loves Oya. His stutter has prevented him from being anything more to her than a cute, "brotherly" type of man, but things are changing.

Acting Note: This play is written in such a way as the actors speak their stage directions. When speaking the stage directions, the actors should do it in character. There is no delineation/parenthetical markings to tell you where the stage directions are, you must simply be be aware of the change in delivery/context.

TIME & PLACE:

The distant present. La Pere, Louisiana. Oya's home.

OGUN SIZE: *(Enter Ogun Size)* I . . . I . . . know . . . I know
that that you can he-hear me,
S-So I'm I'm just standing here talking.
Standing h-here speaking to you, my h-heart.
Y . . . You don't know . . . You s-so blind
If you as-ask me.
I ain't n-never said nothing
Like that to you b-but how you think it make m-me make
me
. . . You ain't neva let me love you, but you gon lay
down
And get closer to death? Snuggle up to him!
Death with his stale breath don't know you like I do.
He just a nasty ol man been looking at you since you was
Was a lil girl. But I been loving you always.
I been in love with your light and your sad eyes.
And I got this home inside me I know I do . . .
My outside seem like it's fragile but in here
A big man that will wrap you in love, Oya.
You come home with Ogun. Just come home.
You let me take care of you for a while.
I'll make it all right. I'll make it okay.

IN THE RED AND BROWN WATER

Tarell Alvin McCraney

AMERICAN SOUTHERN
MONOLOGUE
1 M

THE PLAY:

The first in the trilogy of Brother/Sister plays, *In the Red and Brown Water* introduces us to a community in San Pere, Louisiana. This first story is primarily centered on Oya, a young woman with a bright future in the sport of track and field. When a "man from state" comes to offer her the chance to attend his school on a scholarship, she must regretfully decline due to her mother's illness. After her mother dies, it is too late to attend the school as they have already given the scholarship to the next girl on the list. With no college, no mother, and no one to help her maneuver the tricky waters of young adulthood, she falls prey to the local "ladies man," Shango. After he abandons her, she marries the safe man, Ogun Size. The pang of childlessness, the desire for the man who left her and the slow realization that she is stuck in the life she's living serve to drive her insane.

THE MONOLOGUE:

Shango (twenties) has returned. In some way, his presence only serves to tease and torture Oya because he is really going to marry another girl he has already impregnated, again. He comes to say goodbye and to tell her about the day he had in church.

Acting Note: This play is written in such a way as the actors speak their stage directions. When speaking the stage directions, the actors should do it in character. There is no delineation/parenthetical markings to tell you where the stage directions are, you must simply be be aware of the change in delivery/context.

TIME & PLACE:

The distant present. La Pere, Louisiana. Oya's home.

SHANGO: Yeah, that's why the church going so long.
   They praying for his monkey ass.
   Choir just up there singing.
   Elegua came in to the church and she mad
   As hell. You can tell 'cause her wig all
   Tilted to the side and she walking that
   Big girl walk towards the altar. She
   Talk to the secretary of the mother's board, Mother
   Pickalo.
   Whatever Elegua telling her making her shake and put
   down her head.
   She starts praying. I'm like, "What the hell's going on?"
   Elegua walk up to the choirstand and she just
   Start beating on Oshoosi. Beat beat beat . . .
   All the way down the aisle of the church and out
   The front door. Mother Pickalo, she stands up like she bout
   to declare war.
   She standing there you know in the church lady stance
   You know with her face fully forward Holy Ghost filled,
   Double chin jangling. Gon talk about, "Giving honor to
   God, yall I have some news, you
   know times is hard.
   And the devil is out there I know!" People "Amen-ing"
   and "Yes Lordin."
   I'm like I wish this chick would come the hell on
   And stop the testimony . . . But you know she crying:
   "And Lord the devil can sometimes sneak in here
   Too . . . This holy sanctuary. Lordie G Lord!
   This temple . . . this house of God can be sacked with
   wasteful . . .
   There was money being stolen from
   Out the mouth of God and being used
   To play in some corner crap game
   Filled with wicked youthful derision. Lord God Lord
   God.
   I ask that this money be prayed over and
   Put back into the rightful hands of the church
   So it can pay for the pastor's sons' gonorrhea of the
   mouth!"

Kimberly Mohne Hill   289

INSURRECTION: HOLDING HISTORY

Robert O'Hara

AMERICAN SOUTHERN
MONOLOGUE
1 M

THE PLAY:

Ron's great-great-grandfather is a miraculous 189 years
old. When his family gathers for his birthday party, his great-
great-grandson seems distracted, wrestling with the demands
of his life at Columbia. When Ron goes to say goodbye to his
"gramps"—a man who has been silent for over 75 year—he
hears the old man ask him to "take me home."Thus begins a
physical (and metaphysical) journey for Ron and his gramps, TJ,
back in time to the days of Nat Turner and southern slavery. Ron
gets to live and witness "first-hand" the story his great-great-
grandfather lived as young man. He begins to see, through the
events of the time leading up to Nat Turner's Revolt, that he is
not simply writing a paper for a class about slavery, but he is
writing "his-story."

THE MONOLOGUE:

Ron (twenties) has been celebrating his great-great-
grandfather's 189th birthday. As he readies himself to leave, his
"gramps" touches on a hot-button issue Ron has been enduring
—the writing of his PhD Thesis on Slave Revolutions. As his
gramps chides him for having a "busy brain," Ron's emotions
spill over.

TIME & PLACE:

Somewhere in Virginia. Present-day. Night time. After the
birthday party.

RON: yes. "this thesis than"! for some reason i got it in my
      crazy head that Nat Turner was IT. i mean who the hell
      needs another paper on slavery . . . no offense. *(lit. quick)*
      yeah, iii don't know where it came from but i can't git it
      outta my head and i have nothing new to say about him or
      slavery there's nothing new about the fact that he lost his
      mind and started slashin' folks and okay we survived OKAY
      ALREADY i mean so what throughout history millions of
      people have survived horrible events and american slavery
      is MINUTE when you think about it in terms of what hap-
      pened during the Crusades and even the uh i don't know i
      mean turner's revolt was NUTHIN compared to how those
      brothas and sistas were kickin' up in Haiti okay nat turner/
      slavery BIG DEAL move on but it won't let me Go!!!
      fuck!
      i'm sorry gramps! . . . . sorry i . . . listen i need to get back
      to new york get back to my books so—

INSURRECTION: HOLDING HISTORY

Robert O'Hara

AMERICAN SOUTHERN
MONOLOGUE
1 M

THE PLAY:

Ron's great-great-grandfather is a miraculous 189 years old. When his family gathers for his birthday party, his great-great-grandson seems distracted, wrestling with the demands of his life at Columbia. When Ron goes to say goodbye to his "gramps" —a man who has been silent for over 75 years—he hears the old man ask him to "take me home." Thus begins a physical (and metaphysical) journey for Ron and his gramps, TJ, back in time to the days of Nat Turner and southern slavery. Ron gets to live and witness "first-hand" the story his great-great-grandfather lived as young man. He begins to see, through the events of the time leading up to Nat Turner's Revolt, that he is not simply writing a paper for a class about slavery, but he is writing "his-story."

THE MONOLOGUE:

After traveling back in time to the plantation where his great-great-grandfather, TJ, was a slave, Ron becomes immersed in the day-to-day operations on the plantation. His 20th Century freedom and education are revealed in his vocal outcry against the beating he witnesses on the plantation, causing *him* to be strapped to the beating pole where his great-great-grandfather has been ordered to whip him. After one strike on his grandson's back, TJ (now twenties), turns the whip on the Overseer and kills him instead. His grandson released, TJ tries to teach him they way things are in this time period.

(Note: Strong, emotionally-laden vocabulary is used in this monologue. While oft-used in the time period, the actor/class/group should be aware of the sensitive nature of the language and be prepared to "debrief" after the monologue is played.)

TIME & PLACE:

August, 1831. Daytime. A plantation in Southhampton, Virginia. Before Nat Turner's revolt.

TJ: that man Ova Seea Jones would've made me kill you boy
you cain't act the same heah as you useta Ronnie these
are different times different people heah Izzie Mae takes
a whippin' everyday boy she gats tough skin she built like
a hoss Ronnie—

    [Ron: (angry) That's because she's treated like one.]
i tol' ya not ta say nuthin' didn't i? I tol' ya you didn't know
"nuthin 'bout nuthin'" and what you go and do?

    [Ron: I tried to help her!]
no you tried ta git kilt!

    [Ron: I thought it was the right thing to do.]
ain't no right in Southhampton boy these niggas heah are
slaves you gat that? and whateva these white folks wanna do
howeva they wanna do it wit whoeva they wanna do it that
make it right.

    [Ron: that's.wrong!]
what the hell did you think you was gonna see som' picture-
book technicolor dream fantasy you on a plantation boy planta-
tions gats slaves white folks treat slaves lak shit and the ones
claim they treat they slaves *good* treat they slaves like *good*
shit so nah you brace up and learn ta shut up o' I'm gon' take
yo' ass back home ratt nah you gat it? . . . do you understand
me Ronnie?

    [Ron: . . . . yes sir.] (beat)
Ronnie you gotta learn yo' place there are times when you say
what you gotta say and there are times when you keep all that
stuff ta ya'self none of these crackers know what Izzie Mae gat
inside her none of 'em don't know what that woman liable ta
com' back wit that's dangerous ya see that what's really scary
you don't treat nobody lak an animal beat 'im starve 'im rape
'im take they young from 'im and 'xpect 'im ta lick yo' paw
once you com' round ta pettin' 'im lak I said Izzie Mae built
lak one of 'em hosses and a hoss'll throw yo' ass offa they
back once they load git too heavy so you ain't gotta worry
none 'bout Izzie Mae that woman might not be able ta pick
her minimum but believe you me she sho 'nough know how
much a load she can carry

    (Silence)
nah let's be gittin' on ta that meetin'

INSURRECTION: HOLDING HISTORY

Robert O'Hara

AMERICAN SOUTHERN
MONOLOGUE
1 M

THE PLAY:

Ron's great-great-grandfather is a miraculous 189 years old. When his family gathers for his birthday party, his great-great-grandson seems distracted, wrestling with the demands of his life at Columbia. When Ron goes to say goodbye to his "gramps" —a man who has been silent for over 75 years—he hears the old man ask him to "take me home."Thus begins a physical (and metaphysical) journey for Ron and his gramps, TJ, back in time to the days of Nat Turner and southern slavery. Ron gets to live and witness "first-hand" the story his great-great-grandfather lived as young man. He begins to see, through the events of the time leading up to Nat Turner's Revolt, that he is not simply writing a paper for a class about slavery, but he is writing "his-story."

THE MONOLOGUE:

Ron was unable to stop Nat Turner from carrying on with his plan, even with his 20th century history book that described the outcome of the revolt. His great-great-grandfather, TJ (twenties), confronts his grandson after the other slaves leave.

(*Note: Strong, emotionally-laden vocabulary is used in this scene. While oft-used in the time period, the actor/class/group should be aware of the sensitive nature of the language and be prepared to "debrief" after the scene is played.*)

TIME & PLACE:

August, 1831. Nighttime. A plantation in Southhampton, Virginia. Before Nat Turner's revolt.

TJ: *(furious)* nah what was all that boy! how come you cain't keep yo' mouth shut!
i LIVED it!!! *(beat)*
slavery.
ends.

ronnie.
HUSH UP!
you know nuthin
you know letters on paper
you know big words
connected ta little ideas
you know nuthin
i killed a man this afternoon
wit'out a thought
wit'out a hesitation
i killed that son of a bitch because it was either him o'
you
and. YOU. mine.
i didn't need no mo' time i didn't need no mo' thinkin' i
didn't have no plan
DEATH ain't nuthin new ta me n' it ain't new ta them
slaves
i LIVED it!!
you. the one Watchin'!
i brought you heah ta learn. ta listen. not change nuthin we
change in oura OWN time.
not. in. othas.
you wake up ev'ry mornin' breathin' the AIR that NAT
TURNER fought fo' you ta breathe and you sleep ev'ry
nite wit no FEAR cuz that crazy. nigga. SHOUTED Out at
the Moon askin' his Gawd fo' a way thru dis trouble and
you think you can show up back heah and BLOCK that!!!
ronnie you are who you are because them people that's gon'
git shot up hung up cut up is what will 'llow you ta enter
them doors of that fancy college ya go ta read them wordy
books and write them thesis papers SEE these niggas heah
cain't understand that ALL they know is that they wanna
be FREE and that's what they plannin' ta DO
So they gon' WIN
they might DIE
but they gon' WIN
You. da Proof.
    (the slave and the free man Clock each other)
slavery.
ends.

AMERICAN SOUTHERN
MONOLOGUE
1 M

THE PLAY:

On a train back to Kentucky from California, a young woman named May encounters a fellow "Kentuckian" who has just been discharged from the Army for medical reasons. Though initially suspicious of his gregarious personality and his "too personal" inquisitions, she slowly warms to him. When he promises to come back to Kentucky to take her to the Nibroc Festival, her romantic hopes rise, but he never shows up. Three years, two cities, a few jobs and relationships later, they find themselves together on May's front porch. As they reconnect and clear the air of past betrayals and prejudices, they begin to realize how truly deeply in love they really are, and they become engaged.

(It should be noted that this is the first in a trilogy of plays about this romantic couple)

THE MONOLOGUE:

Though she seems quiet, stiff, and uninterested in conversation, Raleigh (twenty-one) can't resist trying to charm the young lady in the train car stall. She seems disinterested, but still he persists. Here he reveals his reasons for staying on this train.

TIME & PLACE:

December 28, 1940. A train, somewhere west of Chicago.

RALEIGH: Nope. I'm staying. On the train. Going to New York City. Funny, when I got on, boarded the train, back in Los Angelees, I was going home. Not happy about it, but going home. I got on this train. Thought, I can go anywhere. Chicago, anywhere. No one's expecting me. No one knows I'm coming. Got a uniform still on, got a pass. Anywhere I want to go. I can go anywhere. Thought about Detroit, lots of work in the factories there, my brother-in-law says, but I can go do that anytime . . . Home'll always be there. I got on this train, and the conductor told me that the coffins were being loaded in. That Nathaniel West and F. Scott Fitzgerald were riding the same train as I was. So, don't you see, I can't let that go by. When would something like that ever happen again? And no matter what happens, there will always have been a time that we rode the train together. Things are affected by other things. And I can't let that go by. That I'm on the train with the two greatest writers of this century. And I thought I've just got to stay on this train. Follow those men. This is my chance, my time, and if I don't take it now, don't move right now, not later, now, while I'm supposed to, it'll never happen again.

AMERICAN SOUTHERN
MONOLOGUE
1 M

THE PLAY:

On a train back to Kentucky from California, a young woman named May encounters a fellow "Kentuckian" who has just been discharged from the Army for medical reasons. Though initially suspicious of his gregarious personality and his "too personal" inquisitions, she slowly warms to him. When he promises to come back to Kentucky to take her to the Nibroc Festival, her romantic hopes rise, but he never shows up. Three years, two cities, a few jobs and relationships later, they find themselves together on May's front porch. As they reconnect and clear the air of past betrayals and prejudices, they begin to realize how truly deeply in love they really are, and they become engaged.

(It should be noted that this is the first in a trilogy of plays about this romantic couple)

THE MONOLOGUE:

It's been a year and a half since Raleigh (23) saw May for the first time on the train. Much has happened to their relationship, including him going up to Detroit for work and her discomfort being revealed about his family's social status. There has been a strain on their relationship and a secret he's been keeping from her. As he reveals the details of his secret, his body also begins to betray him.

(The scene actually ends with him in convulsions from his epilepsy, but the monologue has been cut before that. If the actor wishes to incorporate the beginnings of an epileptic seizure into the lines, they would come towards the end of the piece.)

TIME & PLACE:

Summer, 1942. A park in Corbin, Kentucky. Near a bench.

RALEIGH: You don't know what being ashamed is. Ashamed is when you can't go off to war with your buddies. When you're going to be the only one left in town. Ashamed is when you have the fits in front of your sergeant. Ashamed is when you give up on your own dreams to chase after something in a skirt and find out she's not worth running after. Ashamed is when your new girl won't come to supper at your house because your daddy is a cripple. Ashamed is when you run into that girl a year and a half later and you realize what a stupid mule-headed old rooster you've been for ever seeing something in her in the first place. Ashamed is having to come home to a dirt-poor farm and feeling guilty of taking care of your mama and your daddy. And instead of going off to war having to go to Detroit to stand fifteen hours a day on the line in a loud, sweaty dark factory. Ashamed is when the factory doctor tells you you got ep'lepsy.

You better leave now. Better catch your train.

Liars, Thieves, and other Sinners on the Bench

Jo Carson

Americal Southern
Monologue
1 M

THE PLAY:

A collection of vignettes and characters from her site-specific, theatrical, documentary-style performance pieces, *Liars, Thieves . . .* is a collection of some of the most haunting voices and stories that Jo Carson was able to witness. Though based on real conversations, Jo uses theatricality and creativity to depict the very real worlds she observed. These stories allow the actors to simply speak and simply believe. In the simplicity, there is beautiful and meaningful resonance.

THE MONOLOGUE:

A man (any age) sits at an outside table at a restaurant. He gives us the history of the place.

[Note to the actors: It is up to you to do the imagination work on these pieces with regard to the details of the place, the people you are speaking to, and the past that led you up to this moment in time. With no narrative to guide you, the limit is your imagination.]

TIME & PLACE:

Newport News, Viriginia. A restaurant with an outdoor seating area. The present.

THIRD PERSON: This was once a field I plowed. I mean this table, this restaurant sits on land I used to plow. My father before me plowed it, too, raised silage for cows. The business was a dairy, but cows have to be fed. Food is cheaper to raise than to buy.

My father used to say if you waited for perfect weather to plow, it would never get done. He was speaking of this field, but he was speaking to a son who was bad about putting things off. I didn't understand it until it was me deciding when to plow this field, and, of course, I said it to my son who never had the opportunity or the obligation to plow this field, never had to make the decision about when to plow, so never had the bone learning that comes of sitting on a tractor dragging a plow, because the time is right even if conditions aren't.

Once, my father was plowing this field and a salesman showed up. He wasn't much of a man to talk to salesmen to begin with, and he was busy. Plowing Cheddar's. Plowing Office Max. Plowing JC Penney. Plowing Outback's. Plowing Outback. The salesman came into the field—the gate was over close to where the Toys R Us is now—stood there waiting while my father drove the tractor with the plow behind it around the whole field, it was a big field, through Barnes & Noble, through Don Pablo's Mexican Restaurant, through the mall, could be forty-five minutes once around, and the salesman started waving when he got close, and my father waved back and kept on. Man was still there when he came around again. My father waved again and kept on again. Salesman gave up. My father plowed until after sunset by the lights on the tractor to get it done. Next day, you do the same thing with a disk to break up clods and then you can plant. You drive the tractor around again to harvest. After the zoning changed and taxes got high, it was me being plowed. The restaurant should be named Progress. Selling the land was not an option. I had to. I don't begrudge people homes and a way of life. I don't begrudge it at all, and heavens knows, I got fair trade for the land. And so many more people live here now. Things cannot stay the same, and I can't make them, don't want to. I even like good restaurants. But sometimes I do miss the gentle, sisterly company of those cows.

AMERICAN SOUTHERN
MONOLOGUE
1 M

THE PLAY:

A collection of vignettes and characters from her site-specific, theatrical, documentary-style performance pieces, *Liars, Thieves . . .* is a collection of some of the most haunting voices and stories that Jo Carson was able to witness. Though based on real conversations, Jo uses theatricality and creativity to depict the very real worlds she observed. These stories allow the actors to simply speak and simply believe. In the simplicity, there is beautiful and meaningful resonance.

THE MONOLOGUE:

A man (any age) tells us about the last time he was given a whipping by his father.

[*Note to the actors: It is up to you to do the imagination work on these pieces with regard to the details of the place, the people you are speaking to, and the past that led you up to this moment in time. With no narrative to guide you, the limit is your imagination.*]

TIME & PLACE:

Newport News, Viriginia. The present.

YOUNG MAN: The last whipping I ever got was a whipping
    I gave. I was about thirteen, I had been messing with the
    battery setup at the barn. I knew I wasn't supposed to, and
    worse, I had fouled the works. I knew I was in for a whip-
    ping, too. My father sent me out to get my own switch.
    And when I brought it back in, I tried to hand it to him.
    He said:
    "No, you're going to whip me."
    "I can't do that."
    "Yes, you can."
    And he bent over. I couldn't do it.
    "Hit me."
    "I don't want to."
    "Do it."
    He made me whip him, like he would have whipped me. It
    took a long time because I didn't want to, but he wouldn't
    let me go without really doing it. I was crying worse than
    if I was being whipped. I've never done anything since that
    made me feel quite so bad. I threw up and he still wouldn't
    let me quit. When he finally stood up he said:
    "How does that make you feel?"
    "Awful."
    "That's how I feel every time I have to whip you. So, please,
    don't do things that make me have to do it . . ."

AMERICAN SOUTHERN
MONOLOGUE
1 M

THE PLAY:

Though the words "Hurricane Katrina" are never used in this play to describe the storm that has left the characters sitting on a roof surrounded by water, the date, setting, and circumstances will clearly draw the reader/audience to make that connection. A reformed addict-turned religious man, Malcom, shares a rooftop with E-Z, a disenchanted, angry young man. Also sharing the rooftop is the corpse of E-Z's friend, Lowboy, who drowned as the waters rose in the neighborhood. As the situation becomes more and more desperate, and the men become more and more dehydrated, hallucinations and drastic measures occur.

THE MONOLOGUE:

Having been on the rooftop for an indeterminate amount of days (less than 3 but more than 1), E-Z (twenties) and Malcom have already held a "funeral" for the corpse of Lowboy, have played innumerable games of 20 questions, and have passed the time with the banal (counting roof tiles) and the meaningful (conversations about life, death and redemption). Here, E-Z reminisces about another time in his life when the circumstances were quite similar.

TIME & PLACE:

A rooftop in New Orleans. August 2005. Late afternoon.

E-Z: Shit. This is somethin', ain't it? This. Right now. This situation we in. Reminds me of this time, this field trip we went on when I was a kid. Out to the swamp. We all on those boats—you know? Those ones with the big fans? Fly on top of the water? Right. So we all on these boats and we stop on this little island for lunch. Some park ranger man is tellin' us 'bout nature, 'bout the crocs and what not, the birds, all the animals all 'round. But I gotta take myself a crap. I mean *real* bad. So I go on over into some trees a way's off, so nobody don't see me, and I take my crap, wipe my ass with a leaf and shit. Problem is, when I come back all the kids, the boats, they gone. There I am on this little island, ain't no one around. So I figure I just wait, you know? Can't be long 'fore they figure I'm missin'. But shit, man, an hour goes by, then another and another. Sun starts goin' down. I'm scared to death, little kid like me all alone in the swamp there. But after a while I come to like the place. Like I got my very own island all to myself. Like I'm the king of this island and can't no one tell me what to do. Figure I can get some branches together, make myself a nice little hut. Make some fishing line outta the vines and shit. Weave myself some baskets outta the marsh grass to collect me some rainwater. Live there till I'm an ole man. Dig my own grave and lie down in it my day come to die. I start hopin' they don't never find me. Just leave me right where I am. Like I'm a king, you know? King of this island an' it ain't nobody's but mine. *(E-Z chuckles. A pause)* Yeah man, they find me.

AMERICAN SOUTHERN
MONOLOGUE
1 M

THE PLAY:

A sequel to *The Last Train to Nibroc,* here we get to see the continued journey of the young couple—May and Raleigh—as they start their married life. The war has come to the front steps of May's family home when her younger brother re-enlists for a second tour after being sent home with an injury from his first tour. Surely, they wouldn't send him to Normandy . . . Meanwhile, Raleigh's writing career faces rejection after rejection and May loses her esteemed position as school principal to the men returning from the war. As they endure the stresses and strains of a young married couple and the pressures of the outside world, their relationship shows its strength when May, selflessly, encourages Raleigh to leave their small town and go to live in New York in order to start his writing career off in a real way.

THE MONOLOGUE:

Freshly home from their honeymoon, Raleigh (twenties) and May have some explaining to do. They were supposed to be in Rock City, but they missed the train when May twisted her ankle. They ended up in a little hotel in Cincinnati, but Raleigh's mother doesn't know that. To keep the charade going, he brings her back a "souvenir" from "Rock City."

(Note: $2.00 in 1944 is the equivalent of about $26.00 in 2012)

TIME & PLACE:

The front porch of a modest home in Kentucky. May's parent's house, where May and Raleigh live with her parents. June, 1944.

RALEIGH: Well, my mom's always wanted one of those bird-houses. And next to our rooming house in Cincinnati, there just happens to be this man hanging a brand new birdhouse from his tree. So I go over and say, mister, I'll give you a dollar for that birdhouse. And he says, that he's not in the birdhouse business. Well, I can't hardly keep from laughing, 'cause he's being so serious about our transaction. When I finally catch my breath I tell him my momma wants a birdhouse real bad. And he says, son, I don't like making birdhouses and if I let you have this birdhouse I'm gonna have t'make another one. And I'm biting my lip just to keep from laughing in his face, 'cause he's so serious. And I nod, like I understand how hard it is to make a birdhouse, and I look down at the ground for a minute, shaking my head all sad like, and I look at the birdhouse again like I'm thinkin' real hard and then I look that old man in the face. I tell him, Mister, I'll give you *two* dollars for that birdhouse if you'll paint "See Rock City" on the roof of it and sell it to me. And that feller looks me up and down and says "mighty expensive birdhouse, son. But if you're just stupid enough to pay two dollars for it, well, then I'm just smart enough to sell it to you." So my mom's gonna have her birdhouse with "See Rock City" on it.

Kimberly Mohne Hill   307

AMERICAN SOUTHERN
MONOLOGUE
1 M

THE PLAY:
A collection of vignettes and characters from her site-specific, theatrical, documentary-style performance pieces, *stories I ain't told nobody yet* is a collection of some of the most haunting voices and stories that Jo Carson was able to witness. Though based on real conversations, Jo uses theatricality and creativity to depict the very real worlds she observed. These stories allow the actors to simply speak and simply believe. In the simplicity, there is beautiful and meaningful resonance.

THE MONOLOGUE:
Male (forties) reveals the effects of racism in the south.

[Note to the actors: It is up to you to do the imagination work on these pieces with regard to the details of the place, the people you are speaking to, and the past that led you up to this moment in time. With no narrative to guide you, the limit is your imagination.]

TIME & PLACE:
Present day. East Tennessee.

21:   The first time I sat in a restaurant where blacks were not served Martin Luther King was still alive. I knew I would not be served; I knew it would be me who served time in jail. I had taken a shower and eaten my lunch in preparation. When I came to consciousness I had vomited my lunch, I had been beaten and handcuffed to the bars of a cell in the city jail. I stayed in that position for a week. I had a wound on my head that needed medical attention. It was not the last time I sat where blacks were not served. I did it until I was sentenced to the federal pen or the U.S. Army, my choice, and I served in Vietnam.

M.L.K. was murdered twenty years ago. My daughter is almost the age I was and we were sitting in a restaurant where blacks are not served. There was no sign that said white only, there was a waitress who behaved as though she could not see us. "We're color blind in America," my daughter said and we walked out.

Black people already know this story and who else do I think might listen—the woman who refused to see us? the couple who came in after we did who were served when we were not? This story is not newsworthy, nobody needed stitches, but this is the same story as the one that cracked my head open. The only thing that changed is the law.

THE WHIPPING MAN

Matthew Lopez

AMERICAN SOUTHERN
MONOLOGUE
1 M

THE PLAY:
Set in the "ruins of a once grand home near Richmond, Virginia" the day after the Confederate Army surrendered at Appomattox and two days before Lincoln's assassination. An old slave, a young former slave, and their young former master reunite at the old plantation to begin their new lives. Old secrets, new injuries and a new societal order leave them all struggling to find their place.

THE MONOLOGUE:
John (twenties) was a slave in the home of the Jewish-Southern DeLeon family. Now that the war has ended and there is a new way of life on the horizon, he confronts his war-wounded, ex-master (and, unbeknownst to him, his half-brother) about his reasons for abandoning the faith in which he was raised.

TIME & PLACE:
Evening. Friday, April 14, 1865. A rainy night in Richmond, Virginia. The former DeLeon plantation. The parlor. After dinner.

JOHN: I taught myself how to read. Your mama taught me "ABCDEFG" and by the time she got to "H," your father had already put a stop to it.

That's not why she stopped. She was so happy to teach me to read. Mrs. DeLeon wanted me to be able to read the Torah, which I did. Adam and Eve. Cain and Abel. King Solomon. King David. And, of course, Moses. The more I read, the more questions I asked. Questions she didn't always have an answer for. Like, when was God going to set us free like he did the slaves in Egypt? Or whether Nat Turner was our new Moses. You ever read Leviticus? "Both thy bondman and thy bondmaids, which thou shalt have, shall be of the heathen that are round about you; of them shall ye buy bondmen and bondmaids. They shall be your possession and ye shall take them for your children to inherit for themselves. They shall be your bondmen forever. But over your brethren, the children of Israel, ye shall not rule."

That's when she stopped teaching me to read. Because I asked the simple yet obvious question: were we Jews or were we slaves? Because, if Simon and I were Jews, that seems to set your family's claim to faith directly against ours, doesn't it?
    [Caleb: If you care to view the world in those kinds of absolutes.]
I was absolutely a slave. You were absolutely my master. You could absolutely discard all that you believe in. Because it was yours to discard if you wanted to. It was never ours. It was given to us and it could be taken away with just some careful reading of Leviticus.

Matthew Lopez

AMERICAN SOUTHERN
MONOLOGUE
1 M

THE PLAY:

Set in the "ruins of a once grand home near Richmond, Virginia" the day after the Confederate Army surrendered at Appomattox and two days before Lincoln's assassination. An old slave, a young former slave and their young former master reunite at the old plantation to begin their new lives. Old secrets, new injuries and a new societal order leave them all struggling to find their place.

THE MONOLOGUE:

When Simon, the devoted ex-slave questions why John (twenties) is acting so bitter and angry towards Caleb (his secret half-brother), John tells him about the first time he was ever sent to the "whipping man."

TIME & PLACE:

Evening. Friday, April 14, 1865. A rainy night in Richmond, Virginia. The former DeLeon plantation. The parlor. After dinner.

JOHN: It wasn't a friendship, Simon. Not when one friend owns the other. Orders him around. Sends him off for whippings.

(The air goes out of the room.)

[SIMON: We ain't talking about whippings.]

Why not? We're talking about everything else. Why, if we were a family, did we get whipped like all the other slaves in town?

(Pause)

Lizbeth used to say to Sarah and me: "you listen to Mr. DeLeon. You do as you told. Or they gonna send you to the Whipping Man. The Whipping Man gonna take all the skin off your back." He was like the devil, the Whipping Man. Smelled of whiskey, sweat and shit, like he hadn't bathed in years. Probably hadn't. He'd pick up the slaves and put them in chains and take them to his shop. There were blood stains on the walls. And a large collection of bullwhips, too. He used them depending on his mood. First time I was sent there, he used a pearl handled bullwhip.

Didn't he, Caleb?

[CALEB: John, you have said enough.]

Caleb and his father came with me the first time I was sent. Did you know that, Simon?

[SIMON: I did.]

But do you know what happened once we got there?

[CALEB: John.]

Mr. DeLeon felt things were getting too chummy around here between me and Caleb. Between us and the DeLeons. Felt Caleb didn't fully appreciate the true relationship between a master and his slave. So off we all went. To learn.

What happened first, Caleb? You remember?

(No answer from Caleb.)

Caleb and his father stood in the corner and watched as the Whipping Man put me on my knees. Didn't you, Caleb? The Whipping Man took off my shirt. He attached my hands to two leather straps. And I was whipped.

(On "whipped," John stomps the floor with his foot then claps his hands together. The sound he makes is

a rhythmic "boom-smack."
This hurts his injured hand. Perhaps the wound starts
to re-open and bleed a bit through the bandage. But
the pain is worth it to make this point.)
And whipped.
(Boom-smack!)
And whipped.
(Boom-smack!)
And whipped.
(Boom-smack!)
Wasn't I, Caleb?
(Again, no answer.)
Then in the middle of the whipping, I heard Caleb's
voice.
"Stop!" he yelled. "Stop!"
I thought to myself, "Caleb is saving me. Caleb is rescuing
me. Caleb cares about me."
And then I heard Caleb say to his father, "I want to do it
myself."
The Whipping Man handed Caleb the pearl-handled bull-
whip. And Caleb whipped me.
Didn't you, Caleb? You whipped me.
(Boom-SMACK!)
And whipped me.
(Boom-SMACK!)
And whipped me.
(Boom-SMACK!)
(Boom-SMACK!)
(Boom-SMACK!)
(John walks to Caleb and crouches down in his face.
They stare at one another for a moment.)
That's when we stopped being as close as you remember,
Simon.

CLASSROOM
EXERCISES

These are improvisation exercises that I often use in my classes or coaching sessions in order to allow the students the opportunity to truly "inhabit" the dialect without needing the words of the script. It is important to remember that improvisation can be scary for many students and the "permission to fail" needs to be modeled at the very beginning of the lesson. Play along!

SMELLY-SEXY-FUNNY (OR BRITISH TEA PARTY)

Four people participate each time—a host and three guests. The situation is a British Tea Party. The host has invited three people over. While the actors are waiting to come into the scene, they each (in their own heads, secretly) endow the other players in the scene with one of the qualities mentioned in the title. The objective is to remain in character and interact with each other while still considering the endowments. It is important to keep the endowments a secret-walking in and saying "you are sooo funny" gives it away too quickly. Many times, the person Actor A has chosen as his "Sexy" will have chosen him as her "Smelly" and the instant physical relationship is fun to watch! The director/teacher can side-coach and cue the actors for entrances and exits. The director can also throw out phrases such as "Make your 'Smelly' 100 times *more* smelly."At the end of the party, when the guests have all left, ask the audience to guess who was who to each of the actors.

(This is, by far, the most popular of all the improvisations that we use. It was taught to me by the folks at Bay Area TheatreSports, and it works for any of the dialects!)

STATUS MIXER

To help tap into the status hierarchy that can exist in plays written about the British, this exercise equates levels of status to numbers. Number 1 equals the lowest status and number 10 equals the highest status. A basic conversation about status characteristics will help the actors acquire the appropriate physical and verbal carriage during the scenes. In general, low status behaviors can include a lack of eye contact, constant appeasement, verbal hesitation (ummms, ahhhs), moving of hands, touching of face, etc. In general, high status behaviors can include steady and firm handshakes, clear speech, unwavering eye contact, poise/stillness, and a demanding demeanor.

Have the actors walk through the room and call out a number. Have them embody that number. Then call out another number and have them change physically to adapt to the new number. Continue to call out different numbers to give them an opportunity to explore many status options and physicalities. Finally, ask them to choose a number and keep it secret. Ask them to embody their secret number as best they can and have them begin to "mix"—talk to each other as if at a social function to which they have all been invited. Make sure to make them talk to as many people as they can while still maintaining their number. When they have had enough time to interact with everyone, and without saying their numbers out loud, have them get into groups of "like-numbered" people. When the clusters have formed, ask the 1's to raise their hands. The 2's? The 3's? And so on. They will tend to have become very good at realizing who was close to them in status numbers.

Status Conversations

An alteration of the Mixer is to have two people have a conversation and each of them starts with the opposite status number (i.e., one of them is a '10' and the other is a '1'). During the course of the conversation, they must slowly move through the numbers and adjust their status accordingly so that, at one point, they will both be at "5" and then they will end opposite of where they started.

(For more information and detail about teaching "Status" in improvisation, see Keith Johnstone's book, *Impro*.)

Character One Minute Ramble

In a circle and with the teacher timing the exercise, each student stands up and speaks for a solid minute in dialect and in *character*, about anything that comes to mind. Though they only have a minute, they do not need to rush. They should also stay away from simply summarizing the play or scene they are performing. Instead, coach the actor to expand his/her imagination and describe what they (the character) had for breakfast that morning or what they intend to do in five years, etc. The element of a "time pressure" will either be a blessing or a curse to some of the actors!

"CHARACTER BATH"/CHARACTER INTERVIEW

Honestly, I stole this exercise from the fabulous movie, *The Commitments*. In the movie, one of the band members is taking a bath and he pretends he's being interviewed on a famous talk show because his band has suddenly become famous. This exercise, however, does not take place in a bathtub! In pairs, actors will interview each other. When they are the one being interviewed, they must answer the questions *in character*. The interviewer can ask them anything. The conceit of a "talk show" could also be used if that helps. Each interview should last at least five to ten minutes. This exercise helps the actors to connect the voice of the dialect with the imagination of the actor and the clues provided by the script. This is a "character deepening" exercise.

(Any of the other section's exercises can be used here as well)

MONOSYLLABIC WORD-AT-A-TIME STORY

In pairs, actors take turns telling a story using only one word at a time. For example, Partner A says "Once," Partner B says "upon," etc. The catch in this version of the word-at-a-time story is that the actors must only use monosyllabic words when they speak. At a certain point, the director can call out "get to the moral of the story" and the actors complete a moral —"the-moral -of-the-story-is - . . . ." They are to use this as a dialect warm-up. This exercise came to me through TheatreSports.

TWO-WORD AT A TIME STORY

Same concept as a word-at-a-time story except that now the participants can string two words together when it is their turn to speak. It should flow a bit faster and allow them a bit more time to incorporate the dialect into their speech pattern without allowing them to get into an inflection pattern yet.

IRISH GROUP THERAPY

I call this "Group Therapy" though it was originally taught to me as "Scene without I/You" (again, at TheatreSports). The placement of this game in the Irish section serves the purpose, through a "verbal restriction" game, to help the actors over-come the tendency to get into an inflection pattern in the Irish dialect.

The construct is this: 4 participants are onstage at all times . . . even when one is "eliminated."When one is eliminated, an-other audience member immediately takes their place on stage. I like to start out as the Therapist just to get the scene going, but I, too, will fail and get eliminated at some point! The Therapist sits in a chair and has the other 3 patients take their positions on the couch/chairs. It is the Therapist's jobs to give everyone names. All actors on the stage (including the Therapist) play the scene as if they have all come to Group Therapy . . . except that when they speak, they **cannot say** "*I, Me, My, Myself, Mine, You, Your, Yours, Y'all,* or *Yourself.*"Ever. If they accidently say one of the forbidden words, they are "out" and must gracefully leave the stage-leaving a seat open for the next member of the audience to step in. When the entire class has had an opportunity to participate at least once, the game can end . . . but most people want a second chance!

PASS THE NARRATIVE

A classic theater game, this one is to be done in the Irish accent and perhaps even incorporate local "Irish" lore!

In a circle, the students tell a story that they make up on the spot. The first person starts the story and sets the stage. When they feel they've said enough, the look at the person sitting next to them in the circle and "pass" the story to them. The next person picks up the story where the first person left off, and so forth. As the story goes around the circle, remember to remind the students to make it consistent with what came before (some students will want to take a "dramatic" tangent for the sake of laughter) and to make the story make sense. The last person finalizes the story and gives it a moral.

DUBLIN MONOLOGUE (PREVIOUSLY CALLED "GALWAY MONOLOGUE")

A member of the group gets an ordinary object from an audience member and sets it down on a chair onstage. Then, one at a time, group members come to the chair, hold up the object, and sit down and talk about its relevance in their lives. The object may be a book, for example, but the monologist can make the object anything he/she wants it to be (i.e. while holding the book, the monologist can begin "I got this pack of gum at this little shop in Dublin . . . "). Monologues should be done for authenticity in the Irish dialect-rhythm, inflection and sound changes should be the focus-not necessarily for humor. The monologist finishes his/her story after about a minute, puts the object back on the chair, and allows another class member to take the stage to do a different monologue using the same object. The monologues are completely improvised. Actors do not need to add on to each other's stories, but it is often very rewarding to hear an earlier story reincorporated into a current story. Everyone in the group should get a chance to rotate through the exercise.

LIMERICK LINE

The students line up facing each other. Following the pattern of the limerick, they make up a poem, one line per student. The limerick pattern is: AA BB A. Below is an example of a limerick pattern:

There once was a very shy girl
Who never set eyes on the Earl
But one day she glanced
At the man as he danced
And he sent her heart all awhirl.

(Any of the other section's exercises can be used here as well)

SOUND BALL INTO GIBBERISH BALL

In a large circle, the teacher throws an imaginary ball to someone. When the ball is thrown, the teacher also makes a sound. The person catching the ball must repeat the sound that was thrown. After catching the ball, that person then throws a new sound/ball to someone else in the circle. As the group becomes especially adept at catching the sounds and sending new ones along, the teacher can add balls.

After a round of simple sounds, the teacher can now ask the students to throw a "gibberish" word with the imaginary ball. Gibberish is a made-up language. It is merely a collection of sounds in no particular order. Though it may resemble a language (my gibberish tends to sound vaguely Scandinavian or Russian), it should not actually be any foreign language. If people are hesitant to try it, have them start simple by repeating "buh-duh-guh" over and over. Gibberish Ball is the same as Sound Ball except it has gibberish words instead of sounds.

GIBBERISH GIFT EXCHANGE

In pairs, Student A gives Student B an imaginary gift. Student B holds it and "observes" the shape and size and weight of it. S/he can talk about it. When s/he opens the gift, s/he should describe it and have a reaction to it. S/he should use it the way it is meant to be used. S/he should say thank you. And then s/he should repeat the gesture by giving Student A a gift. *The entire exercise is done in gibberish . . . no English at all!*

CAFÉ WITH TRANSLATORS

This exercise requires two actors, sitting at a coffee shop and two "translators," standing upstage of the actors. It is important that the translators maintain a completely inactive face/expression throughout the exercise. They are solely responsible for translating into English (with a Latina/o dialect) the words that the actors will be speaking. The actors will be having a conversation . . . in gibberish. After Latina/o #1 speaks in gibberish, Translator #1 translates what was said in Latina/o-accented

English. Then, Latina/o #2 responds in gibberish and Translator #2 translates. The conversation continues in this pattern until it reaches a natural conclusion, then the speakers and translators switch places.

African Continent Improvisation Exercises

(Any of the other section's exercises can be used here as well)

All in the Timing (with a nod to David Ives)

A bell or the ability to say "switch" is necessary for this exercise . . . though I prefer the bell. Two actors are having a conversation in English (with an African continent dialect). When the teacher rings the bell, they must seamlessly revert to speaking in gibberish. When the bell rings again, they revert back to English and the story should have progressed. If the director wants, the bell could signify only *one* actor's switch between gibberish and English, and the word "switch" could cue the other actor . . . that way, the scene could conceivably have one person speaking English while the partner responds in gibberish.

Animal Family Dinner

Because many of the scenes or plays in the African Continent section deal with anthropomorphic characters (animals that act like people or have human qualities . . . like speech), it may be important to take the fear out of playing an animal character. This exercise is designed to do just that.

Start with a simple walk around the room. Let the actors discover how their own body tends to move through space. Have them discover their "center"—the part that seems to lead them. Then call out directions to change their center; side coach them to walk while leading with the head, or the nose, or the knees, or the hips, etc. Get them used to moving in a way that is not familiar. When they have done this, the director can then add characteristics of various animals in the side coaching commands. Examples include: walk like an elephant, move like a Meer cat, move like a lion, etc. After this has been done, attach attitudes or qualities to the animals such as: move like a caffeinated squirrel, or drink like a thirsty hummingbird, or walk like a sweaty bear.

After the call and response portion of the exercise has been done for enough time, direct the actors to choose one of the animals/attitudes that they just did and put it back into their bodies. Have them move throughout the room. Have them look at the other animals in the room with them. Have them now

Kimberly Mohne Hill 325

adapt the physicality/attitude to be present, but subtle inside their bodies. Have them keep it as a part of them, but secret—as if they could walk down the street just like any person would, but with the subtle characteristics of their animal. Have them think of what the voice of this person would sound like. What would their name be, etc?

After everyone has a clearly established animal persona living inside them, have them circle up and introduce themselves to the group.

Keeping the characteristics in mind, in groups of four or five, have the actors perform an improvised "family dinner."Side coach them to reveal more or less of their animal nature throughout the scene. Give all the actors in class a chance to participate in their own dinner scenes.

AFRICAN CONTINENT IMPROVISATION EXERCISES
(Any of the other section's exercises can be used here as well)

I AM REALLY A LION
This is primarily a subtext-type game that can be used in an improvised scene or as an exercise to do with text/scenes.

In advance, the teacher writes out a bunch of different animals on slips of paper which the students will draw out of a hat before their turn. It is good to have a number of animals with vastly different physicalities so the scenes can be varied. For example, try to avoid having only "cat-like" animals. Mix it up.

The students draw an animal card and that becomes the character that they *secretly* are playing. They should not make any obviously animal-like movements (i.e. licking their hands and rubbing their heads to wash themselves), but rather, they should focus on the subtle nuances that lie underneath the animal's demeanor—the energy of a squirrel, the blindness of a bat, the clumsiness of an elephant in a small room, etc.

With this animal characteristic in mind, have them play their scripted or improvised scenes. Remind them to listen to their partners and respond to their partners (they can become a little too invested in themselves in this exercise). At the end of the scene, ask them to tell the group which animal *their partner* was during the scene.

(Most of the other section's exercises can be used here as well)

SOUTHERN STORY-STORY-DIE

Standing in a straight line, shoulder to shoulder, about 6 to 8 actors participate in this exercise. It is an "elimination" exercise, so at one point, there will only be one person standing.

The teachers points to a person. While the teacher is pointing at that person, that person is telling a story (in dialect). The teacher then switches, quickly, and points to someone else in the line. As soon as the teacher points to the other person, the first person stops talking (sometimes mid-word) and then next person must pick up the story *exactly* where it left off. For example: Kristin begins the story with "*Jonas was a great fa—*" and the teacher points to Kenzie who must then say, "*—ther. He loved his family more than anything.*" The teacher continues to switch the storytellers by pointing at different people in the line.

A person gets eliminated when:

1   They do not pick the story up exactly. i.e. Kristin says "*Jonas was a great fa—*" and Kenzie says "*a great father.*" (Kenzie repeated a couple of words.)

2   They make grammatical errors. i.e. Kenzie says "*Jasmine was talking and . . .*" and Kristin says "*and she is home.*"

3   They hesitate.

4   They say something that makes no sense to the flow of the story or is completely unrelated to the preceding sentences.

When people get eliminated, they sit down in the audience and a new story is started.

SOUTHERN TAG MONOLOGUE

One person stands up and begins an improvised monologue (in a Southern dialect, naturally). When another person wants to take over, they simply tag the previous speaker and continue the story without skipping a beat—even if the speaker stops in mid-sentence. This can continue until the entire class has had a chance to participate or until the monologue reaches a natural conclusion.

Special Thanks and Acknowledgements:

Santa Clara University's Department of Theater and Dance, Santa Clara University's College of Arts and Sciences Dean's Office, Craig Slaight, Deborah Sussel, American Conservatory Theater, Aldo Billingslea, Barbara Murray, Michael Bates, Courtney Mohler, Elan Amaral, Molly Murphy, Monique Hafen, Marc Jacobs, Dawn-Elin Fraser, VASTA, Kat Koppett, Bay Area TheatreSports, Abby Hardin at Drama Books NY, Patsy Rodenburg, Elizabeth Brodersen, Susan Thrasher, Loris and Doug Puckering, all of my students, past, present and future, my daughters Kristin and Kenzie and most especially, my amazing husband and partner in this labor of love, Dave Hill.